# Right or Reconciled?

*God's Heart*
*for Reconciliation*

# Right or Reconciled?

*God's Heart*
*for Reconciliation*

Joseph L. Garlington

**Destiny Image® Publishers, Inc.**
**P.O. Box 310**
**Shippensburg, PA 17257-0310**

"Speaking to the Purposes of God for This Generation
and for the Generations to Come"

ISBN 0-7684-2004-0

For Worldwide Distribution
Printed in the U.S.A.

This book and all other Destiny Image, Revival Press,
and Treasure House books are available
at Christian bookstores and distributors worldwide.

For a U.S. bookstore nearest you, call **1-800-722-6774**.
For more information on foreign distributors, call **717-532-3040**.
Or reach us on the Internet: **http://www.reapernet.com**

# Dedication

To Barbara Jean, my wife and partner, who has willingly shared the message of this book in our marriage, in our family, and in our church. I have learned more from you and your unconditional love than from all the books and messages I have ever read or heard on this subject. Thank you for your faithfulness and your unswerving devotion to your first love, King Jesus, and to me.

# Acknowledgments

To live above with the saints we love, that would be
    glory,
But to dwell below, with the ones we know, now that's
    a different story.[1]

The writer of Proverbs says, "He who separates himself
seeks his own desire, he quarrels against all sound wisdom"
(Prov. 18:1). You can't live a life with a view toward the message of reconciliation in isolation. It takes other people who
are willing to share that journey with you. I owe much to some
who joined me early in this process. We dared to believe—
together—that blacks and white could worship, live, love, and
learn together.

I am indebted to these who pioneered with me. They
were the "early adopters" of the complexities of this message. We were all experimenting when it wasn't popular in
the early 1970's, and I am enjoying the fruit of our collec-
tive labor and sometimes painful discoveries. Thank you,
Dale and Eunice; Dennis, Gayle, Michael, and Jean Louise;
and John and Kathy.

I owe a special debt of gratitude to Chett, Joey, Dana, Ly-
dia, Kip, Shauna, and Benita, our children, who at various

1. My paraphrase from a popular hymn.

times—then and now—allowed our home to be the laboratory for great experiments in human relationships. They believed what Barbara and I taught, and became "models" of reconciliation in their own right. Just one spectacular result of all this is a treasury of nine beautiful grandchildren, many of them biracial, who have added an incredible measure to our "quiver." Truly, "It is the blessing of the Lord that makes rich, and He adds no sorrow to it" (Prov. 10:22).

# Contents

# Foreword

I am never surprised to discover something new and good about Joseph Garlington—not any more.

But, when I first met Joseph over two decades ago, I was surprised. I was surprised to discover the rich blend of spiritual passion and intellectual acumen present there. He was an example of a balance that one hopes for, yet which I could hardly remember ever finding in the scope and breadth that was revealed in this man.

A few years passed.

During that time, I saw Joseph rather infrequently. We would occasionally pass one another at a conference, or I would see him pictured in a magazine. These were the "bumping-into-one-another-at-an-airport" type of contacts. But then another moment came...

I knew of a need for a top-caliber speaker to fill a key slot at an event, and I made a call. "Let me tell you about a guy," I said. "Do you know Joseph Garlington?"

They didn't.

So I proceeded to describe my convictions regarding Joseph, and as I did so, I noted the silence on the other end of the line. Although no one voiced it, I recognized the understandable presence of doubt, of an idea that I was exaggerating—that no one could be this good. However, the individuals invited him anyway, and it became *their* turn to be surprised. Later, it was *my* turn again, not to feel surprise, but to feel a warm satisfaction that bordered upon smugness when they reported to me: "Wow, thanks! Joseph was everything you said!"

Besides Joseph's depth and breadth—spiritually and in ministry—I am regularly moved by his sensitivity in leading worship, his musical skill as a soloist and composer, and his remarkable, incisive use of humor. He's a man of rare boldness and humility, as well as genuine godliness that is devoid of pharisaical prudishness. He is as unabashed to maintain a vulnerability to the supernatural moving of the Holy Spirit as he is to challenge and confront the superficial or fanatical in such settings. In short, without flattery or hyperbole, he's Joseph Garlington: Renaissance man.

One more thing.

I can write this because it won't change him. He's a realist—about himself, first; then about other things that we all face today, important things. As you take this book in hand, he is about to lead you along lines of thought about one of today's *most* important things. As he does, you can be sure that Joseph isn't going to try to dazzle you with fancy footwork; he's too honest. Nor will you be bored with the impractical or merely ideological; he's too real.

He's writing to cut to the core of an issue that's central to the heart of God at this present moment of history—now as never before. And as you pursue this theme with Joseph, I have a prediction: You'll be touched deeply and moved spiritually.

And, let me add, when you are—when you find the Holy Spirit probing, stirring, and reshaping areas of your soul—two more things will happen. First, you'll be glad you met Joseph Garlington. And second…

I won't be surprised.

Jack W. Hayford
Pastor, The Church on the Way
President, The King's Seminary
Los Angeles, California
March, 1998

# Introduction

A single statement, in the context of one's life, can bring focus and immediate clarity to questions you have had for most of your adult life. It was that way for me one Sunday morning in Rochester, New York. I was attending a conference at my younger brother Paul's church. My oldest brother John was the speaker that morning. I enjoyed listening to John; he was always eloquent, insightful, and humorous. At any moment he could suddenly transition—without warning—to an incredible prophetic mode and it was always exciting when he did this.

While I was giving rapt attention to what he was saying, I was also pondering, as I had been for several months, some real concerns about the direction of my life and the future course of my ministry. There were critical questions I needed answers to, and I had come to the conference with the hope that I would hear something that would help me to bring direction to my coming years of ministry. I needed to believe that I had invested my time and energy creatively, and that any future investment would have eternal value to it.

Suddenly, my brother stopped—in the middle of his message—and he began speaking to me as though he had been listening to my heart thoughts. He said:

"Joseph, you have been concerned about the way you have spent your past few years in ministry, and whether or not the time you have invested was worth it. But like Joseph of old, God has brought you this way to teach you how to walk in integrity, and to learn the language of the Egyptians and the Hebrews."

I was stunned! In one broad stroke, God had given me a paradigm through which I could view the entire sweep of my life. A paradigm is a way of seeing things, and if it is a *principled* paradigm, it will affect the entirety of your life. I was cross-cultural. I was meant to move between worlds and cultures, and I had been in the Father's "School of Ambassadors" for plenipotentiaries. (A plenipotentiary is a person who has full authorization to represent the government.)

At this point in my life, it really is apparent that the "Jesus method" of teaching is the usual one. Luke wrote in the Book of Acts, "...all that Jesus began to *do* and *teach*" (Acts 1:1). Notice the order: first it's do and *then* it's teach. I like to say, "First He *does* you, and then He teaches you what He's been doing to you." My brother's words—in one fell swoop—put into perspective much of my life's journey. On so many occasions, I was the lone black face in a sea of white faces, whether it was elementary school, in high school, or in many ministry settings. I hadn't chosen to be the "token" anything, but often that was the case.

Several years ago, my wife and I purchased an automobile model that we had never owned before. We couldn't recall ever "seeing" this model before we owned one, but once we were owners, we saw them everywhere! In the same way, many of the great truths of Scripture are often lived, or experienced, before they are understood, or "rationally assimilated." I am suggesting that it is the living of the "experience" that enables you to "see" what you could not see prior to the experience. This is the underlying foundation of the message of this book.

Reconciliation must be *lived*; it can't be just "studied." Western society, particularly American society, is notorious for studies. We pay millions for the studies, and then throw away the results. The Bible is not just a book to be studied, but rather to be obeyed. We think that we examine Scripture, but in reality Scripture examines *us*. One day, Jesus informed His disciples that it may be necessary at times to forgive a brother seven times in a single day! The stunned disciples responded with a plea to the Lord to "increase [their] faith." Jesus answered their plea with a teaching on servanthood and obedience. (See Luke 17:1-10.)

Moses told the children of Israel that they were to remember all the ways that the Lord had led them. He indicated that the course of the journey itself and the experiences along the way were designed by God to instruct them and to teach them dependence upon God. As I "remember" the way, I am convinced that my calling was to be a "peacemaker" and that my burden was to help others—especially the Church—to see that we have an obligation to communicate the *Father's* heart for all His people, and not just our own.

I can live with the pain of racial rejection, gender rejection, or religious rejection, but the only way to truly overcome is to become a "minister of reconciliation." The only truly authorized medium of this message is the Church of Jesus. If we don't do it, we will live with the consequences of our disobedience. The Church must rise above her identity in ethnicity and gender, above denominationalism and sectarianism, and get on with the business of making disciples of all the nations. It's going to take the whole Church to reach the whole world, and that world is cross-racial and cross-cultural. If we don't do it, the consequences are even more frightening than one would want to contemplate.

There are many who believe that the message of this book is very improbable, given the nature of the makeup of our present situation in the Church world. But I have had the joy of pastoring a church and working with other pastors who have the same heart for this message, and in the past 15 years, we have produced credible models of church life where people really do get along. May the Father of lights help you find such a church and people who want to live this message.

# Chapter 1

# **Right or Reconciled?**

**Who Do You Have to Hate?**

God is calling us to be reconciled with Him, but many people insist that God or somebody claiming to represent God has "done them wrong." Many years ago, before Barbara and I moved to Pittsburgh, we both had the opportunity to get some additional training at Fuller Theological Seminary. We took classes together, studied Greek together, and generally had a wonderful time. We developed some rituals during that time that were quite nice. For instance, if I had a morning class one day and Barbara didn't, then she would send me off with a warm kiss and a prayer. But one particular morning just before I left for an early class, Barbara's keen sense of fashion sounded an alarm of some sort (everything must match in her universe whereas mine is perfectly happy in the "eclectic" or "anything goes" mode most of the time).

Barbara looked at me and said, "*Why are you wearing that?*" Now men handle this kind of thing better when you say, "That's the dumbest combination I've ever seen you wear." But when you turn it into a question and say, "Why are you wearing that?" then you're asking for a "rationale that is associated with your particular combination of color exchanges," and you're really raising questions about "Are you a 'summer' or 'winter' personality? Don't you know that 'summer' and 'winter' don't mix those kinds of combinations?" In other words, I took her comment as an attack, and went into my male G.I. Joe mode (which means I counterattacked).

I said, "Well, why are you always criticizing what I put on?" She said, "I'm *not* always criticizing you," and I answered, "Yes you are! You do it all the time." And she replied, "I *don't* do it all the time," and our fellowship "intensified" as we continued to exchange comments with increasing volume. (I didn't remember the verse that says, "A gentle answer turns away wrath, but a harsh word stirs up anger" [see Prov. 15:1], and I wasn't interested in giving a soft answer anyway.)

I thought, *Hey, I don't have to put up with this,* and I decided to hold Barbara at a distance from my life. I remained polite enough to still enjoy her cooking, but I remained aloof. Finally I came to her and said, "Barbara, I really need to talk with you," and she said, "Sure." I took the wrong approach and said, "A wall has *grown up* between us...." Now she knew as well as I did that walls don't "grow" up between people—people have to *build* them, but I didn't want to take responsibility for this wall. I recalled what had taken place and explained in detail how I had been offended by her responses to me (after all, don't women like details?). "You said this, and then I said this, and so forth." I concluded by saying, "I just can't live with this." She listened to the whole thing while I bared my heart, and I thought, *This is God. This is really God. I'm getting through, and this thing is gonna be settled in just a few minutes.* I was getting set for the apology.

Barbara waited patiently until I was totally finished, and then she said, "Honey, are you finished?" And I said, "Yes." Then she said, "I never said those words that you said I said." And I replied, "O-o-o-h, you said them all right. You said them." She said, "Honey, I didn't say those words, and here's one of the reasons why I *know* I didn't say them. It's because

*I honor you too much* to say what you say I said." I thought, *Oh man....* You see, I knew that part of her argument was right! Barbara did honor me.

When she threw the "honor" card into the game, I thought, *I'm stuck now. Could I have been mad for three weeks for nothing?* Now I didn't want to admit that I'd been mad for three weeks for nothing, so I was saying to the Lord, "No, no, she said it. God, just bring it back to her memory. You can do it. She believes in dreams and visions. Give her a dream tonight." I was praying hard. That night I went to sleep in the other room because I really wanted to seek God and get real clear on this problem...

I sought Him with all my heart, but He didn't say anything to me. At five o'clock in the morning, I knew I was going to have to face her again. Normally Barbara would "give in first," but it didn't happen this time and I knew I was in trouble. So that morning, I said, "God, what am I going to do? I believe I'm right; she believes she's right. I think she's wrong, and I know You know she's wrong, but You won't help me." Then He asked me the question, "***Do you want to be right, or do you want to be reconciled?***" As much as I hated the question, I knew the answer.

When I was born again, whether I liked it or not, you became my brother or sister. The chances are that if I had met you in those early days, I wouldn't have liked you at all, but there wasn't anything that I could do about it. The truth is that when I first surrendered to Jesus, I hated white people. I was born and raised in the public housing projects of Buffalo, New York, to a family that was essentially poor (although we didn't know that we were poor).

By the time I made it to Howard University in Washington, D.C., I knew that I was poor, but my professors told me to say I was "culturally deprived." I also learned a lot of other fancy ways to say that I was poor, but they didn't do a thing to change my economic status. When I left, I was still poor.

My life experience made me think that it was okay to feel such hatred toward white people. One day the Lord confronted me with it, and I said, "Lord, I really don't want to feel this way." At the time, I was preaching as a guest evangelist for a church in Los Angeles, California. This large black congregation had a total of three white members. When I finished my sermon, a little white lady with gray hair and a beautiful smile came up to me. I was cradling my Bible in one hand and I had my other arm down at my side, and this little lady just put her arms around me and pinned my arms to my sides. Then she began to say, "I just love you, Brother Garlington."

I said, "Praise God," but at the same time I was doing my best to break free. That woman had a steel grip on me, though, and she wasn't about to let go. She said, "You remind me of my son." I thought to myself, *You are lying. I know I don't remind you of your son.* She kept right on holding me. I was still wearing the clerical robe I'd worn for the service, and the perspiration I'd generated during the ministry time was making me feel cold. Then that woman started crying and telling me that she wanted me to be her son, and my kindly response was a silent but urgent prayer, *God, get me out of here!*

The woman just kept hanging on to me and telling me how the message had ministered to her. All of a sudden I felt something begin to seep out of me. When the lady finally let go of me, I realized that I *felt differently* about her than before she had come up to me. In fact, I felt differently about other white people too. I began to understand that this woman really was my mother in this New Jerusalem. I remembered the Scripture passage where Jesus promised us, "And everyone who has left houses or brothers or sisters or father or mother or children or farms for My name's sake, shall receive many times as much, and shall inherit eternal life" (Mt. 19:29). I have mothers all over the world, and they come in all colors. When I see them today, I don't view them according to the flesh because I don't know them that way anymore.

> *We are not again commending ourselves to you but are giving you an occasion to be proud of us, **that you may have an answer for those who take pride in appearance, and not in heart**. ... For the love of Christ controls us, having concluded this, that one died for all, therefore all died; and He died for all, that they who live should no longer live for themselves, but for Him who died and rose again on their behalf. Therefore **from now on we recognize no man according to the flesh**; even though we have known Christ according to the flesh, yet now we know Him thus no longer. Therefore if any man is in Christ, he is a new creature; the old things passed away; behold, new things have come* (2 Corinthians 5:12,14-17).

When you know people "according to the flesh," then what you see in the flesh will work in you to activate whatever hostility you have in you toward others. God wants you to know people by the spirit, not by the flesh.

Who do you have to hate in order to get along in society? If you are in management, do you hate people in labor? If you are a dues-paying union member, do you hate non-union people? One of the brothers in the church said that whenever he had to service the account of one particular American company based in Pittsburgh, he couldn't drive his foreign car onto their lot. Why? Because they say, "The Japanese are the ones who are stealing our markets and taking our jobs." I remember hearing people say in the 1950's, "Don't buy Japanese goods—they are low quality goods. They're cheap." Today, when you say something is made by the Japanese, it means it is high in quality and perhaps high in price too. Who do you have to hate?

## Do I Have to Hate My Podiatrist?

My wife and I had a friend who was a podiatrist, a medical doctor with specialized training to work on feet and toes and anything else below the ankle. He was a great guy and a Spirit-filled Christian who loved Jesus. On one occasion, my wife had to have some surgery done on her feet and she went to an orthopedic surgeon for a second opinion. During the examination, she explained that our podiatrist had already recommended a minor surgical procedure, saying, "I need to adjust your toes with a little surgery. I'll just go in and remove a portion of the bone in both of your little toes because that's what is causing your continuing problem with painful corns."

When Barbara shared this, the orthopedic surgeon said, "Who told you that?" He simply dismissed the podiatrist's advice and said, "Really, I can do the same thing by just shaving off all the area where your corns keep appearing." Of course that seemed to be the better operation in comparison to a procedure requiring someone to open up the toe and remove a piece of bone. Barbara consented to the second doctor's procedure, and I even watched it for a while until my head started to swim. But right after the surgery, the orthopedic surgeon came in and said, "Now *if this doesn't work...*" Of course you know the rest of the story. In the end, Barbara had to go in and have the bone removed just like the podiatrist had said in the first place.

This story isn't meant to be a put-down of orthopedic surgeons or a promotion of podiatrists—it is an illustration of the way we are expected to make stark, unyielding choices between options that shouldn't involve hatred or enmity at all. One day I was riding in a car with my friend the podiatrist, so I told him the story about Barbara's feet and I asked him, "Is there real antipathy between orthopedic surgeons and podiatrists?" I don't know what my friend thought antipathy meant, but he said, "No, *they just hate each other.*"

I can think of another sore spot involving health care. Some of our best friends are chiropractors and some are medical doctors. It seems to me that the only medical doctors we know who actually like chiropractors are Christians. My realm of knowledge is relatively small, but chiropractors have been so maligned in our society that when you say "chiropractor," most people start to twitch. Yet when I ask any crowd of people, "How many of you have ever been helped by a chiropractor?" I always see a huge percentage of them raise their hands. When I ask the same group, "How many of you have been helped by a medical doctor?" almost every hand in the house goes up. Isn't that wonderful? I like to ask them, "Which one did you have to hate to go to the other one?" You don't, do you?

If you are a Serbian in Yugoslavia, are you required to hate Croatians? If you are a member of the Xhosa tribe in South Africa, are you required to hate all members of the Zulu tribe? If you are a Democrat, is it essential that you actually hate Republicans? Or if you are a man, are you required to continually put down women? If you are a woman, how do you talk about men when you are in the company of other women? How do black people talk about white people when there are no white people around? How do white folks discuss black folks when there are no black folks around? How do Italian people talk about Polish people when there are no Polish people nearby?

**God Has Given Us a Ministry**

> *Now all these things are from God, who reconciled us to Himself through Christ, and **gave us the ministry of reconciliation**, namely, that God was in Christ reconciling the world to Himself, not counting their trespasses against them, and **He has committed to us the word of reconciliation**. Therefore, we are ambassadors for Christ, **as though God**

***were entreating through us;*** *we beg you on behalf of Christ, be reconciled to God* (2 Corinthians 5:18-20).

There are two words in this passage that deserve special attention. The Greek word translated as "ministers," *diakonia,* and the word *reconciliation.* I loosely translate *diakonia* to mean "the *service* of deacons." God has made all of us *deacons of reconciliation.*

So God was "in Christ reconciling Christians to Himself...." Wait a minute. Did you notice something odd about that statement? Does the verse say God was reconciling Christians or *the world?* When you read that passage, did you think "world" or "us"? The Bible says God was reconciling *the world* to Himself. God was in Christ reconciling you before you ever wanted to be reconciled!

## If God Was a Republican

If God was a card-carrying member of America's Republican Party, He would become reconciled with the Democratic Party! Then He would reconcile with the Independent Party. If He was a member of England's Labour Party, He would reconcile with the Conservative Party there. The fact is that we can't expect God to join us and our political parties or private agendas—He commands *all of us* to be reconciled to Him!

Was Jesus conservative? Yes. Was He liberal? Yes. Was He radical? Yes. Was He a heretic? To some people, yes. Jesus came to earth and began to upset everything the devil had worked so hard to accomplish among sinful men. Jesus upset religious leaders and institutions in His day, and He still triggers more hostile responses in our day than any other person in the history of mankind. Yet throughout His ministry He was concerned about only one thing: He was determined to obey His Father by reconciling the world to Himself.

God the Father told Jesus, "I want You to go down to earth for Me. Do You see that guy who cheats people by collecting more taxes than he is supposed to? I want You to go and make friends with him. Okay, do You see those prostitutes over there? Go make friends with them too. Do You see those people standing on the street corner praying loudly in their choir robes? Stay away from them; they are religious. They call themselves Pharisees, but I call them hypocrites. Just hang out with the sinners, Son. You will be okay." God was in Christ, and Christ was in the world.

Twenty years ago, I preached a message entitled, "Stop the World, I Want to Get Off." I was really interested in Jesus' coming to get me out of here, but He hasn't stopped the world yet and I'm still here. It is like He is saying, "Garlington, if you want it to get better, then *make it* better." When I asked how I was supposed to do that, I discovered two commissions that we have as Christians. (There are more than two, of course, but I'm just going to focus on two.) Jesus has called us to be *light* and to be *salt*.

Light illuminates and rules the darkness, and salt affects everything that it comes into contact with. Salt also provokes thirst. If you take the living Christ with you and begin to live among unsaved people, then sooner or later they will get really thirsty. The more you hang out with them, the thirstier they will get. "You got any water?" "Yes, but it's living water." "I'll take any kind you've got right now, just as long as I can get this salty taste out of my mouth." God has given you and I the same ministry that Jesus had, and that is the ministry of reconciliation. Unfortunately, we don't act like it.

All my life I was taught in the church that friendship with the world is enmity with God, so I thought I couldn't have any friends who weren't Christians. We spent all our lives witnessing to Christians, and Sunday after Sunday, we thought we all needed to get saved again. (It's called "being born again, again.") We had countless altar calls for people who "weren't saved enough" this week so they could come and get saved all over again. Since none of us knew any sinners, we couldn't invite them to church and none of them got saved. We were the embodiment of the old poem that says, "Lord, bless me and my wife, and my son and his wife; us four and no more in Acts 2 and 4."

We used to worry a lot about smoking because it was one of the seven major sins in our church. Yes, smokers could come around you all day as long as they had some mints available to mask the fragrance of hellfire on their breath. They could come right up to you and talk as long as no one could tell that they had been smoking. But if they happened to forget their toothbrush or pack of Lifesavers, and got too close when they said, "Praise the Lord," someone might smell the telltale odor of Raleighs or Marlboros on their breath. Brother, they were going to hell that very moment. And if they somehow didn't go to hell, we were shocked that the earth didn't open up and swallow them.

Yet in the same meeting, chances were good that the preachers had gathered together before and after the meeting to talk about other preachers. These respected men of God would run down a fellow minister in one breath, and then with their next step, they would rise before the congregation and give a mighty shout of "Praise the Lord." They felt that they were safe though because nobody could smell the hellish odor of slander on their breath. (God knows, though, that you can't use Lifesavers to erase it.)

How can we take up God's call to be reconciled to the world when we are having such a difficult time being reconciled to any brother in Christ who just happens to be the "wrong color" or have the wrong accent because he lives south or north of the Mason-Dixon line? (The Mason-Dixon line was an imaginary boundary between the state borders of Maryland and Pennsylvania that was a symbolic dividing line between pro-slavery states choosing to secede from the Union and the generally anti-slavery states that remained in it in the American Civil War that followed. Even to this day, it remains a symbol of division between "the South," or the former Confederate States, and "the North.")

It took me a long time to accept the fact that who I am doesn't make any difference *in* Christ. It only makes a difference when you are *outside* of Christ.

*For you are all sons of God through faith in Christ Jesus. For all of you who were baptized into Christ have clothed yourselves with Christ. There is neither Jew nor Greek, there is neither slave nor free man, there is neither male nor female; for you are all one in Christ Jesus. And if you belong to Christ, then you are Abraham's offspring, heirs according to promise* (Galatians 3:26-29).

Paul tells us that in Christ "there is neither Jew nor Greek" (there are no racial distinctions), "there is neither slave nor free man" (there are no socioeconomic class distinctions), and "there is neither male nor female" (there are no gender distinctions).

When God came to earth, He chose to hang out with sinners. He had the reputation of being a friend of sinners (see Mt. 11:19). What would happen to you if someone heard that you were a friend of sinners? The first thing your "Christian critics" would say might be, "Well, birds of a feather flock together, you know." Nevertheless, God was in Christ reconciling the world to Himself. I want you to read several verses from Paul's Epistle to the Galatians, and pay special attention to the final verse.

*Tell me, you who want to be under the law, do you not listen to the law? For it is written that Abraham had two sons, one by the bondwoman and one by the free woman. But the son by the bondwoman was born according to the flesh, and the son by the free woman through the promise. This is allegorically speaking: **for these women are two covenants,** one proceeding from Mount Sinai bearing children who are to be slaves; she is Hagar. Now this Hagar is Mount Sinai in*

*Arabia, and corresponds to the present Jerusalem, for she is
in slavery with her children. But the Jerusalem above is free;
she is our mother* (Galatians 4:21-26).

We have the same mother. I don't care whether you are
German, Italian, Brazilian, French, Zulu, Hottentot, Norwe-
gian, Spanish, Irish, or Martian—we have the same mother
in Christ. Male, female, or still in question, once you receive
Christ Jesus as Lord and Savior, we have the same mother.
Isn't that amazing? We have the same mother, and we are all
*free*, whether or not we realize it.

Who is it that you are required to hate in this life? Everything changes when God comes to you and says, "You have
a new mother. Your mother is My heavenly Jerusalem, My
Kingdom, and it is above. That means you are free, and you
can no longer make decisions after the flesh." Your decisions about life and death, and love and hate, must be made
in the Spirit from this point on.

Don't make the mistake of thinking that I'm talking
about politics or some social program or agenda. This is a
message on what we must do with the ministry of reconciliation. What has God given us? What has He called us to be,
and how can we fulfill our calling out in the world without
fumbling around for answers? So God has made you a minister or deacon of reconciliation. Now sir, what do you do
when people tell degrading jokes about women? Do you
laugh, or do you speak up and say, "Guys, I can't join in
that"? Ma'am, what do you do when you hear someone tell a
demeaning story about an ethnic group? What do you say?
Paul gives us a simple guideline in the Book of Ephesians:
"Let no unwholesome word proceed from your mouth,
but only such a word as is good for edification according
to the need of the moment, that it may give grace to those
who hear" (Eph. 4:29).

When I was "evangelizing" some 20 years ago (*evangelizing* is a religious code word for traveling around from church to church preaching to the saved), I came home from one of my trips and opened the door to my apartment to find that my TV and my clothes were gone. I was really concerned about it. Actually, I was upset about it. No, I was distraught. (I'm sharing with you some more of the fine words that I learned in the university, but I could also give you some other words that I learned in the projects that would *really* tell you how I felt about the situation.)

Let's just say I was deeply impacted by that experience. If I had arrived soon enough to see one of the "brothers" (a colloquial term for an African-American male commonly used by African-Americans, for those unfamiliar with American slang) walking down the street with *my TV* in his hands, I would not necessarily have called him a "brother." I had come to a point in my life when my alignments could no longer be strictly laid out on a racial, social, or gender basis. The truth is that our "mother" is above the heavens. She is free, and we share the same mother in our Kingdom covenant with Christ Jesus.

## Saying It Is Easier Than Doing It

I remember the time I phoned a man who is now a very good friend of mine and the pastor of a very large church in one of America's largest cities. At the time this African-American man, who was and is an outstanding preacher, was still pursuing advanced studies in seminary. I was asked to call him with an invitation to speak at a large regional conference. I said, "Dr. So and So, we have heard good things about you and your ministry."

My phone voice probably made me sound like I was "of the Caucasian persuasion," and in retrospect this man was very gracious during this call from a total stranger. He agreed to come to the conference, and when this man actually had the opportunity to meet me in person, he looked at me and said, "Brother, if I had known you were a brother, I would have said, 'Yes, I'll come!' right away. But I didn't know who you were." My friend's reaction was typical of our reactions throughout the Body of Christ, and it is something that I deal with personally as well. My friend is not a racist; he is a gracious and godly man of the utmost integrity. He is a very gifted and highly educated man. His reaction simply illustrates the way that we sometimes feel more comfortable with our "own kind." It is natural for a woman to feel excited when she sees another woman in the Body of Christ moving in the gifts and the power and glory of God. It is not like a woman is no longer a woman simply because she surrenders her life to Christ. Nor is it true that a black man ceases to be a black man when he enters the Kingdom. The problem is simply this: *We need to realize that God has drawn a much larger circle for "our kind" than we have.* We need to adjust our lives, thoughts, and behavior accordingly.

When I watch the Olympic Games, it doesn't make any difference whether I'm watching a woman, a man, a teenager, a white American, a Japanese American, or an African-American. As long as they are wearing "the red, white, and blue," I cheer for them! Even when a "white guy" from America battles it out in the boxing ring with a "black guy" from Africa, I will still root for America. Now that is a limited analogy, but seriously, our family ties broaden and grow richer when we enter the family of God. That's where the lifeline is, and you share a common blood bond in Christ that is vastly superior to ethnicity, gender, and class ties.

Many times we have a difficult time assimilating all that God is saying to us about our new family, because this changeover doesn't happen instantly. When I first became a Christian, I still had some strongly negative feelings about people of certain colors and races. It didn't change overnight, but it did *begin* to change. The Holy Spirit began to do something inside me, and He began moving me inexorably toward the path of love and acceptance of others. He had His hand in my back, moving me step by step toward true reconciliation and unity.

God knows that we have a tendency to believe the strange idea that we can cut ourselves off from other parts of the Body and still be the Church. We're especially bad about this if we think we have the tiniest shred of justification. Many Christians and non-Christians point to the felony conviction of former American televangelist Jim Bakker in 1989 as proof that some people "don't belong" in the family of God.

We may not like what Mr. Bakker did, but anyone with a brain must admit that Jim Bakker didn't do the damage done by Ivan Boesky, a former Wall Street marketeer convicted of insider trading in 1987. He defrauded investors of $200 million and was fined $100 million. He received a three-year sentence and served only 22 months in a white-collar prison and four months in a Brooklyn halfway house.[1] Yet nobody talked about putting him behind bars for eight years. After all, he wasn't a Christian.

Mr. Bakker, on the other hand, was given the most severe sentence the judge could legally hand down for overselling "Lifetime Partnerships" in his PTL Heritage USA real estate and family entertainment complex. Many have said that Bakker essentially "overbooked a hotel" much as airlines routinely overbook their flights. I don't subscribe to many of his practices and deeds in the 1980's, but it was also hard for me to reconcile the severity of Mr. Bakker's sentence when I see convicted rapists and murderers routinely released early from ten-year sentences! Mr. Bakker was finally released after serving five years of his eight-year sentence, but many Christians are still invoking their "right" to separate themselves from this repentant brother. God is asking us: Do you want to be *right* or *reconciled*?

We need to stop allowing the world to tell us how to be Christians. Jesus said that the disciple is not greater than his master (see Jn. 13:16), so we need to remember how the world treated Christ. We all have the same mother in Christ. We can't say, "Well, he just doesn't act like one of our family." That's tough. You have the *same mother*, and you can't divorce yourself from that fact.

The moment you say, "I love Jesus," the news media will label you as a "born-again Christian," which is meant to permanently link you to every professing Christian who has ever sinned, fallen, or made a mistake in public view. I don't like to be put into a box by people, but if I'm going to be put in there, then I will say, "Now watch me, and I'll show you what a born-again Christian is like. You may have a different idea about what he or she is like, but if you are going to label me, then I'm going to break out of your box! I'm going to tell you that God sent me here to reconcile *even you* to Himself!" Now here is what love does:

> "He drew a circle that shut me out,
>   Heretic, rebel, a thing to flout;
> But love and I had the wit to win.
> We drew a circle that took him in."[2]

Jesus came and essentially said, "I'm here to make some changes, but most of all I'm here to show you that the Father has a different attitude toward the world than that of the Pharisees." Many of us have been stuck with Pharisees all our lives (and some of us have even *been* Pharisees). You can spot a Pharisee by the telltale signs of hypocrisy. Pharisees don't like anybody and they don't appreciate anybody. No matter what or how often you do something good, that kind of Pharisee will find something wrong with it. If you dare to preach a sermon about something like reconciliation, they will tear it apart and say, "Wasn't that a shame what Pastor Garlington preached? Wasn't that a mess?

Where did he get that stuff?" Oops, you just stepped in the puddle of a Pharisee.

Pharisees pray like this: "God, I thank You that I'm not like other people. Thank You for making me better than that poor street person, that alcoholic, and that rotten lost person." The honest truth is that we *are* like them! Countless numbers of Christian men act like misogynists, or "women-haters," while saying they don't hate them. Millions of Christians hate millions of others Christians because they have different skin colors, eat different foods, or say different words over their communion wafers. We need to take personal responsibility for what we have done to one another. First we need to repent and get right with God so we can be reconciled to one another. Then we can reconcile the world to God as well. Paul warned the Corinthian believers:

> *And the eye cannot say to the hand, "I have no need of you"; or again the head to the feet, "I have no need of you." On the contrary, it is much truer that the members of the body which seem to be weaker are necessary; and those members of the body, which we deem less honorable, on these we bestow more abundant honor, and our unseemly members come to have more abundant seemliness, whereas our seemly members have no need of it. But God has so composed the body, giving more abundant honor to that member which lacked, that there should be no division in the body, but that the members should have the same care for one another* (1 Corinthians 12:21-25).

We need to turn to one another and say aloud from our hearts, "I need you." We need to see each other as significant parts of the Body of Christ, and without each part fulfilling his or her God-given call and destiny, we will all be impoverished.

We have been expressly commissioned to go into our world, a world that is hostile to the Word of God, hostile to

Christians in general, and hostile to the purposes of God. The world has its own way of seeing things, and in a way, we can't be upset just because the world doesn't see things like we see them. Our challenge is to make all men see the mystery of a supernatural Church composed of diverse people from different cultures bonded together in love and diversity. Why should society believe that mankind's prejudice and division problems can ever be solved when the Church can't even model unity in Christ with all Heaven's resources at her disposal?

In this season of the Church, the issue isn't, "Who's done wrong?" It isn't "Who has enslaved who" and "Who responded to it," or how much one group has stolen from another. The issue is, *"Do we want to be reconciled?"* The truth is that if we don't want to be reconciled, we won't be. If you insist on being "right," then you can't be reconciled. Even if you are right, you can't insist on it. You have to give up your right to be right. God basically said, "I can kill you or I can die for you. I have the *right* to kill you, but I'm going to give up My right to be right so I can *reconcile you to Myself.* And while I'm doing it, even if you are upset with Me and call Me dirty names, I'm still not going to count your trespasses against you." Jesus made it easy for us to get saved, and it ought to make it easy for us to forgive as well.

I can't stop people from hating each other. (I can't even stop the bickering between my wife's podiatrist and her orthopedic surgeon.) We shouldn't say, "You people shouldn't act like that." We should say, "Be reconciled to God." If we can get people reconciled to God, then He will get them reconciled to each other. When racists hate each other, the Church must model racial reconciliation. In a society of class distinctions, the Church must model a classless society where people are neither bond nor free. When the battle of the sexes rages out of control, the Church must model unity among equals where there is neither male nor female in Christ.

The best way for us to help others is to make the right choice ourselves when the question comes, *"Will you be right or reconciled?"*

### Endnotes

1. Rob Wells, Associated Press article, as reported in the *Lexington* (KY) *Herald-Leader*, (November 14, 1996).

2. Excerpted from the poem, "Outwitted," by Edwin Markham.

# Chapter 2

# Has Your Chicken Been Kicked?

There was a farmer who used to trade chickens for supplies from the owner of the local general supply store. On certain mornings, the farmer and his son would get up at four o'clock in the morning and prepare a dozen live chickens for delivery by tying their feet with light rope or twine. Later in the morning, the farmer would drop off the chickens in the backyard of the supply store and then load up the supplies he needed.

The store owner and his son had a familiar routine too. At around two o'clock in the afternoon, when the store owner's son would come home from school, the father would tell him, "Son, go out and set those chickens free." So the boy would take a sharp knife and walk out to the backyard where the chickens were lying on the ground in the shade. After he cut the ropes around the chickens' legs, they were free for the first time in six or seven hours, but they would still lie there like they were dead because they had been tied up for so long. Even though the ropes that bound them had been removed, they didn't *know* they were free.

At first the boy encouraged the birds to get up by saying, "Chickens, get up. Go! You are untied, and there's food and water over there. Go!" Nevertheless, the chickens just continued to lie on their backs quietly clucking away. By their appearance, everything seemed to be just fine. You would think they had been that way all their lives.

Then the boy heard his father's voice through the back door of the supply store, "Son, what are you doing out there? Did you cut the chickens free?" The boy said, "Yes, Dad."

"Well, what are they doing, son?" the father asked. "They are lying on their backs," the son replied, knowing full well what would come next. When the father said, "Son, get those chickens busy, would you?" he did the part that he liked to do the most after he cut the chickens free each week. He waded into the pile of chickens lying on their backs and began to gently kick them with his feet—just enough to roll them over and startle them out of their deadly slumber. As those chickens found themselves rolling and flying left and right, they suddenly discovered that they were no longer tied up and that they really could walk.

*So it is with the Church.* The Church was tied up for a long time, and then we were set free. But nobody has worked on us enough to make us believe that we really don't have to lie there and take all the abuse of bondage from the enemy of our souls. So we don't move, preferring instead to lie on our backs and cluck softly as if we were born into bondage and will spend all our days bound and on our backs in helpless slumber.

The Father is telling His Son who set us free long ago, "I need You to do some kicking for Me," and He has come down to wade among us and gently (in most cases) kick us like those chickens. We are flying all over the place, and one by one we are suddenly discovering that we don't have to lie there and get kicked. We really can walk. We really can move. We really can fly.

## God Isn't Counting Our Sins

*Now all these things are from God, who reconciled us to Himself through Christ, and gave us the ministry of reconciliation, namely, that God was in Christ reconciling the world to Himself, **not counting their trespasses against them**, and He has committed to us the word of reconciliation. Therefore, we are ambassadors for Christ, as though God were entreating through us; we beg you on behalf of Christ, **be reconciled to God** (2 Corinthians 5:18-20).*

So God was "in Christ reconciling Christians to Himself...." No? Remember, God was reconciling the *world* to Himself. God was in Christ reconciling *you* before you ever wanted to be reconciled! The first step you need to take in the next 60 seconds is to be *reconciled* to God if you aren't already!

Some of the unpleasant things we are experiencing today have come upon us because we have refused to understand the power God has given us in reconciliation. He has loosed something among us that is kicking us all over the place. Tell yourself out loud:

### "If you don't pay attention to what God is saying to you, you may have to get your chicken kicked!"

Have you had your chicken kicked recently? What are you and I supposed to do with this ministry of reconciliation? Underline this answer and memorize it: *In a divided society, the Church must model unity.*

When I was in seminary, we had one teacher who occasionally would say, "This is a very important point." We learned that whenever he said that, *that point was going to come up on a test.* God is telling the Church, "This ministry of reconciliation is a very important point." Now what does that tell you? It is coming up on a test in the very near future.

*For we do not commend ourselves again to you, but give you opportunity to boast on our behalf, that you may have an*

*answer for those who boast in appearance and not in heart.
For if we are beside ourselves, it is for God; or if we are of
sound mind, it is for you.* **For the love of Christ compels
us**... (2 Corinthians 5:12-14 NKJ).

What makes us do the things God commands when we
don't want to do them? The love of Christ *compels* us. So how
can you love your enemy when you would rather not? What
compels you? The love of Christ. (It certainly isn't the enemy
or your good feelings about the person.) Look again at verse
14 and what follows:

*For the love of Christ compels us, because we judge thus:
that if One died for all, then all died; and He died for all,
that those who live should live no longer for themselves, but
for Him who died for them and rose again* (2 Corinthians
5:14-15 NKJ).

### Roll Call for the Breathing

Are you alive? (Check for a pulse if you aren't sure. Some
people might need to put a mirror by their mouths to make
sure that they are breathing.) Seriously, are you in Christ?
Then you no longer have the option of living for yourself.
You and I are to live for Him who died for us and rose again.
As usual in our dealings with God, His blessings for our obedience far outweigh the cost. Verse 16 begins with "Therefore..." When you find a "therefore" in Scripture, find out
what it is there for!

*Therefore* **from now on we recognize no man according
to the flesh***; even though we have known Christ according to the flesh, yet now we know Him thus no longer.
Therefore if any man is in Christ, he is a new creature;
the old things passed away; behold, new things have come*
(2 Corinthians 5:16-17).

Have you noticed that all this activity we are talking
about has a locus or common center point? It all takes place

in or through one sphere, and that is "in Christ." Christians are *in Christ*. "Therefore if any man is *in Christ*, he is a new creature" (2 Cor. 5:17a). One translation says, "he is a new specie." Then there is that wonderful miracle that everyone who has sinned, failed, or made mistakes loves to hear over and over again: "The old things passed away; behold, new things have come" (2 Cor. 5:17b). Look again at what Paul says about our "trespasses":

> *Now all these things are from God, who reconciled us to Himself through Christ, and gave us the ministry of reconciliation, namely, that God was in Christ reconciling the world to Himself,* **not counting their trespasses against them**, *and He has committed to us the word of reconciliation. Therefore, we are ambassadors for Christ, as though God were entreating through us; we beg you on behalf of Christ, be reconciled to God* (2 Corinthians 5:18-20).

Imagine that somebody told you, "I'm going to give you ten mistakes." Now imagine that you have made your ninth mistake and you have only one left before you bottom out. You go to this person and ask, "How many do I have left?" secretly hoping that he won't remember all the mistakes you've already made. How shocked would you be if he said, "Oh, I'm not counting"? That is exactly what God is saying to the world: "I am not counting."

That's our message to the world as Christians: "God isn't counting." He isn't keeping score. He could, but He isn't. We are commissioned to tell sinners, "He is not imputing or indicting you for your sins or violations." Why not? Because He sent Jesus to reconcile us to Himself. On top of that, once we receive Christ and become a new species in Him, He commits this message of reconciliation to us!

### How to Avoid the Boot of Grace

Since you probably don't want to get your chicken kicked, it is important for you to understand how all this happened. You need to discover what God wants you to know so you can get up and get moving now before the swift foot of God's grace boots you into action with a jolt from above. Let's turn again to Paul's Epistle to the Galatians.

> *Tell me, you who want to be under law, do you not listen to the law? For it is written that Abraham had two sons, **one by the bondwoman** and **one by the free woman**. But the son by the bondwoman was born according to the **flesh**, and the son by the free woman through the **promise**. This is allegorically speaking: **for these women are two covenants**, one proceeding from Mount Sinai bearing children who are to be slaves; she is Hagar. Now this Hagar is Mount Sinai in Arabia, and **corresponds to the present Jerusalem**, for she is in **slavery** with her children. **But the Jerusalem above is free; she is our mother*** (Galatians 4:21-26).

Abraham had two sons, a son of human ingenuity named Ishmael and a son of promise named Isaac. Ishmael's mother was Hagar, the Egyptian maid of Sarah, Abraham's wife. In Genesis chapter 16, Sarah decided that since she could not give Abraham a child, she would let Hagar bear a child for her. The modern term for this practice is "surrogate motherhood," but as Solomon said, there really is nothing new under the sun. Surrogate motherhood was actually a legal part of the culture of that time.

So what was the problem? God had promised Abraham that He was going to give him a son through Sarah, but Abraham and Sarah *began to doubt that God would ever do it*. That's when Sarah suggested that they "help God" a little by giving Abraham her servant girl, Hagar, as a second wife. Of course, a baby was born from that union, but *it wasn't the baby that God had promised*. God had another baby in mind for the covenant He had promised, a baby who would not be born until Ishmael was 14 years old (see Gen. 17).

The son "born of the flesh," Ishmael, persecuted the much younger Isaac, the son "born of promise." Sons born in bondage will always persecute those born in freedom. If you get impatient and tired of waiting on God and produce something on your own, then when God finally gives you your promise (and He usually does), your homemade version will persecute and oppose the God-given promise you've been waiting for. That goes for children, careers, relationships, ministries, and dreams—and for anything else that God has promised you.

Paul said that the Ishmael/Isaac conflict is an allegory of the two great covenants of God with man. These are typified in the *earthly Jerusalem* rooted in the covenant of the Law of Moses and the bondage that the Law brings, and the *heavenly Jerusalem* rooted in the "better covenant" in Christ's blood and the freedom we receive through God's covenant of mercy and grace in Christ apart from works.

Before we received Christ as Savior and Lord, *we were all born of the bondwoman.* All of us were sinners until we were saved by grace in Jesus Christ. In that moment, as was pointed out in Chapter 1, we all were born of the same mother, the heavenly Jerusalem of God's supernatural Kingdom.

### We Act Like Chickens Waiting to Be Kicked

Our recurring problem is this: Like those chickens that had to be kicked, we keep acting like our legs are still tied up in the bondage of the Law. We act and think like we are religious slaves who have to perform and work our way into our Master's house, when He has chosen to *adopt* us as His sons and daughters with all the rights and privileges that entails.

There was a bear that spent 12 years in a 12-foot by 12-foot cage. Over the years, he learned to walk from end to end of the cage in a perfect stride, even with his eyes closed. He would go right up to the wall and spin around to march to the other wall. When somebody remarked that the bear was too large for that cage, a new cage was built for him that was three times as large.

When the bear was moved to the new cage, everyone expected the bear to display some excitement and curiosity about his more spacious surroundings. But do you know what that bear did? He began to walk toward the far wall of that new cage, but one-third of the way there he suddenly spun around and returned to his original spot, where he again spun around and advanced one-third of the way into the cage and so on.

Although the bear had 36 feet of free space, he still kept himself confined to an invisible 12-foot by 12-foot area. His body had been moved to a 36-foot by 36-foot cage, but the bear was still living in the same cage that had been his home for 12 years. What was the problem with this bear? It wasn't his new cage. The problem was that the bear had brought his old cage with him! He may have been in a bigger and better cage, but he didn't know it so he didn't enjoy it. Maybe he needed the same remedy the chickens needed…but it's a little tougher finding someone who is willing to motivate a full-grown bear with a swift kick of grace.

God wants the Church to get motivated and walk with Jesus. The problem is that when we were promoted into the unlimited Jerusalem of God's grace through Christ, we brought the legal religious bondage of our old familiar earthly Jerusalem along with us—complete with all its limitations, guilt, and self-destructive thinking patterns. As children of bondage, we were used to living within the limits of culture, ethnicity, gender, class, nationality, politics, economic status, and the slave mentality that affects everything in our lives.

### Will God Have to Kick Our Chickens?

If God has to kick our chickens to help us overcome our mental block of slavery, then He will. The Church—and that includes you and me—needs to abandon her slave mentality and the chains of man's religion and step into the freedom of grace in Jesus Christ. We need to say, "I am part of a Jerusalem that is above, and my mama is free!" Now if your mother is free, then so are you. And remember, *we have the same mother.*

Here is the exciting thing about God's Kingdom: The very people whom God sends out as ambassadors of reconciliation *were just reconciled themselves!* Now the world's governments send people to school for years to learn the diplomatic skills and knowledge required for ambassadors. They carefully choose what to say and what not to say, and when and how to say things. They are so skillful at "nonspeak" that any time you listen to diplomats talk on television interviews, you need interpreters in the room just to translate what they are saying. No one sends unskilled political greenhorns out as ambassadors for the United States, Great Britain, Sweden, or any other country.

"Have you ever done this before, Mr. Garlington?" *No.* "Where were you born?" *In the projects.* "Okay, well, I'm afraid we can't use you at this time." *But I can talk—what do you want me to say? I can handle it.* "But there are certain skills you must learn."

God isn't like man. He is the ultimate risk-taker. He is supremely confident because He is God. He saw the world in all its mess, and He knew it was alienated from Him. According to Paul in the Book of Romans, the world was actually hostile; it was an enemy of God (see Rom. 8:7). In spite of all that, God still loved us and sent His Son to reconcile us to Himself. Let me put it this way:

**God hugs porcupines.**
**Then He sends His porcupines out**
**to tell other porcupines the good news:**
*God hugs porcupines.*

God didn't love us when we were great. He loved us when we were mean, hateful, and nasty. He loved us when we used to spend our weekends burning crosses in people's yards or taking aim at unsuspecting victims in drive-by shootings. He loved us when we were throwing Molotov cocktails during a riot on campus or "in the 'hood." He loved us when we were shoplifting at the five-and-dime store or snatching purses during a church service on Sunday. He loved us when we were falsifying information on the corporate database to get an extra big bonus check or lying to the IRS. He wants to hug us, needles and all!

God has cut away the bands that held us in bondage and somebody needs to tell some of us that we can really walk and fly now. We don't have to steal, strike out, or scam if somebody won't give us a job or a promotion. Why? Because we have the same mother, and our mother is free!

Sometimes God sends the most unusual people along to kick our chickens. The apostle Paul wrote, "I am debtor both to the Greeks and to the Barbarians, both to the wise and to the unwise" (Rom. 1:14 KJV). According to the Greeks of Paul's day, anyone who did not speak Greek was a "barbarian." In our day, we use the term *barbarian* for people who are cruel, vicious, uncultured, and uneducated. When the Roman empire came to dominate Greece, they brought in a "Greco-Roman" prejudice toward anyone who didn't participate in their culture, their pantheon of gods, their literature, poetry, music, or debauched lifestyle. If you weren't in their circle, then you were a "barbarian." Many of us don't want to owe a debt to anybody, but Paul was essentially saying, "If you are a human being, you owe every other human being something as it relates to your existence." He said that he was a debtor both to the Greek and to those who don't speak Greek, to both the wise and the unwise.

There was a very intelligent man with a Ph.D. who was forced to stop his car in front of a mental hospital to change a flat tire. As he put the lug nuts from the flat tire in the hubcap, he accidentally kicked the hubcap and the lug nuts rolled into a large storm drain grate. When he realized that there was no way to recover the lug nuts, he began to pace back and forth asking himself, "What am I going to do?"

Meanwhile, a man who was sitting on a hill overlooking the road watched the whole thing. Finally he walked down to the road and told the stranded man, "Why don't you take a lug nut off of each wheel and put it on the one wheel that has none until you get to a service station?" The pacing Ph.D. suddenly stopped and said, "That is a brilliant idea." Then he remembered where he was and looked closely at the man who had been watching from the hilltop. "Are you a patient there at the mental institution?" he asked. The man nodded and said, "Yeah." When the motorist asked, "What are you doing here?" the man answered, "I'm here because I'm crazy, not stupid."

Many of us don't want to admit that so-called "foolish people" can help us once in a while. The truth is that even if you can hold your own in an argument with philosophers and other more erudite people, and even if you have a vocabulary filled with long complicated words that no one uses anymore, if you don't have common sense, you won't know when to come in out of the rain. Paul openly acknowledged his debt to so-called "barbarians" as well as to educated Greeks. (He didn't want to get his chicken kicked because of pride or arrogance.) We are all debtors.

Some of the most independent people I know live in New York City. Many of these citizens seem to think that they don't need anything from anybody. It was amazing to see how independent New Yorkers reacted during the citywide garbage strike several years ago. They suddenly began to realize that they needed a particular group of people whom they normally didn't even think about. At first, the residents of New York simply watched the garbage pile up on the streets and thought, *They'll give in. They'll be picking up that trash within a week.* But they didn't, and the smell of the rotting garbage began to grow even faster than the towering trash piles cluttering their crowded streets. All of a sudden, officials started to "negotiate" in earnest when angry New Yorkers began to pressure city hall, "Give them anything they want—*but get the garbage out of here!*" Once we get in trouble, we quickly realize we all need help from somebody sometimes.

## The Porcupine Gospel and Barbarians

"For the Scripture says, 'Whoever believes on Him will not be put to shame' " (Rom. 10:11 NKJ). The simple message in this verse is that if you believe on Jesus, you will not be put to shame. Believe it or not, this promise even applies to the person who sells *Penthouse* and *Playboy* magazines at the convenience store. God extends it to the abortionist behind our pro-life picket lines, to the witch next door, and to the man down the street who drinks too much and sometimes beats his wife.

The things that these people do are not wonderful, but God wants to reconcile them to Himself anyway. First God reconciled you to Himself, and then He entrusted His ministry of reconciliation *to you.* The ministry of reconciliation is not reconciling people to you and your views; it is reconciling people to God and His views—including the people you and I consider to be "modern barbarians." We need to remember that we all were lost at one time. Too many of us have forgotten that important fact.

"How are you doing?"

"I've had a bad day. I just had a couple of Pharisees in here a few minutes ago. They really did a number on me."

"I'm sorry to hear that. What did they say?"

"They called me all kinds of names. Told me I was going to hell."

"Listen, I've got some good news for you: *God in Christ isn't counting your sins against you.* I'm here to tell you that I was in worse shape than you are, or just as bad, and He didn't count all that against me. He loves you and He wants to be your friend. All you've got to do is say, 'God, I want Your friendship,' and He'll handle the rest of it."

"Really? That's not what the other guy said. The other guy said if I don't quit selling this stuff, God would burn this place up. Do you suppose that's why he had a Molotov cocktail in his hand at the time?"

Listen—not one of us is authorized to tell people that God hates them. Most people already know that judgment is coming. Just listen to them talk. Most people will tell you, "I just feel like something bad is going to happen." Very few unsaved people feel like something good is going to happen. That's why they flock to those "Get Better" programs by the thousands and willingly lay down $600 to $800 per person to hear somebody somewhere tell them, "It's going to be okay." In the meantime, God has commanded us to give them this clear message free of charge: "Whoever calls on Me will never be put to shame. *Never.*"

The problem is that we're not sure we believe it ourselves. That's why we're getting our chickens kicked.

How about you? Are you tired of getting your chicken kicked? Ask yourself the question, "Do I want to be *right*, or do I want to be *reconciled* to God?" Your answer sets the stage for the rest of your life and for eternity as well.

# Chapter 3

# It's Going to Cost You to Stay With Me

I think Jesus shocked people. I don't think He was good-looking. I think the heavenly Father deliberately disguised Him so no one would be attracted to Him because of external distinctions. When I was growing up, there was a very godly woman whom I loved to be around. She was kind and warm and generous, and she was always reading her Bible. She had a way of getting happy in the Lord at the moment when you least expected it. Sometimes somebody would be preaching and she would shout "Hallelujah!" and scare everybody, but I loved her. I thought she was the most handsome woman I had seen. She was gracious, and she always smelled nice. When you are ten years old and you find somebody like that, it is wonderful. It is like having a third grandmother.

When I was 17 years old, I was traveling with a cynical evangelist who told me that this woman was ugly. I bristled and said, "No, she's not!" He persisted and said, "Have you ever looked at her? She is probably the homeliest woman in the whole organization," but still I defended her. I always looked at her through eyes that loved and cared for her, but one day I looked at her and realized that the evangelist was making an external judgment that would probably be accurate. I had to admit that this woman wouldn't win an average beauty contest, but it wasn't her external beauty that attracted me—*it was what was going on inside her* that drew me and so many others to her.

I imagine that when God the Father talked to Jesus about coming to the earth, He didn't just say, "Go on down there." I think He spelled out the cost of the assignment. "I'll tell You what is going to happen. The men whom I have made are going to kill You without cause, Son. But before they kill You, You are going to wish they had. They are going to say all kinds of ugly things, and even Your earthly brothers are going to turn against You. But You need to get the mission done, Son." Paul says God was in Christ reconciling the world, so Jesus was the Father's agent of reconciliation.

He told Jesus, "Go into this hostile world. Greet, meet, and spend time with hostile people. Spend time with them and give them this message: 'God says, "I still love you." ' They will tell you, 'We don't like You.' " Despite the cost and the shame, Jesus came. And when men rejected Him and His Father, saying, "We don't like You," He answered, "I know," and He opened His arms and bared His heart. That's why He came—to demonstrate how God the Father feels. But Jesus didn't stop there:

> *Now all these things are from God, who reconciled us to Himself through Christ, and* **gave us the ministry of reconciliation**, *namely, that God was in Christ reconciling the world to Himself, not counting their trespasses against them, and* **He has committed to us the word of reconciliation.** *Therefore,* **we are ambassadors for Christ**, *as though God were entreating through us; we beg you on behalf of Christ, be reconciled to God* (2 Corinthians 5:18-20).

## God Says He Isn't Angry With You

An ambassador is "an official envoy; especially a diplomatic agent of the highest rank accredited to a foreign government or sovereign as the resident representative of his own government or sovereign or appointed for a special and often temporary assignment."[1] An ambassador holds a very important office. Once you become an ambassador for a country (or for God's Kingdom), you have to begin living your life for those you represent, not for yourself. As an ambassador for the message of reconciliation, you hold a very important office. You are one of a very special separated group of people in the world who are authorized by the Supreme Sovereign to model unity. You are not authorized to say, "I don't like what is going on here." You are authorized to say what God has told you to say.

We represent the Kingdom of God in a world formerly under the control of the kingdom of darkness. As "ambassador plenipotentiaries," we have full power and authorization to extend God's covenant of love and grace to others. We are authorized to ratify treaties and to tell people, "God in Christ isn't angry with you, and He is not holding anything to your account. Be reconciled to God."

*When therefore it was evening, on that day, the first day of the week, and when the doors were shut where the disciples were, for fear of the Jews, Jesus came and stood in their midst, and said to them, "Peace be with you." And when He had said this,* **He showed them both His hands and His side.** *The disciples therefore rejoiced when they saw the Lord. Jesus therefore said to them again,* **"Peace be with you; as the Father has sent Me, I also send you"** (John 20:19-21).

Let's get these points in our thinking: First of all, God was in Christ when He reconciled us to the Father. Second, God has *given us* the ministry of reconciliation. Third, we are now ambassadors for Christ *representing His interests*, not our own. Fourth, God in Christ is actually pleading through us to the world, "Be reconciled to God."

## Don't Let the Silence Close In

Just as Jesus did before us, we will have to do more than tell the world, "Peace be unto you." People are longing for more than mere words. They are looking for a demonstration of God's love and power. Like the disciples just after Jesus' death and burial, people in the world aren't thinking about great spiritual thoughts or promises. They work, run, play, and indulge their pleasures around the clock. Many people try to stay intoxicated or high on drugs all the time, because if the silence ever closes in, they will have to deal with the faceless fears of death without hope. They are shut in the room of their faithlessness; they are locked in for fear of what they will face when their last breath leaves their bodies. They are not excited at all about "glorious church services, great sermons, or wonderful hymn singing." They are just worried about whether or not they are going to make it through the night. Like Jesus before us, we need to invade their lives in the middle of their fear.

We need to stop reading our Bible religiously and start reading it practically. The passage from the Gospel of John shows us that it wasn't enough for Jesus to tell the frightened disciples, "Peace be unto you." He said, "Will this help, guys? Look at My hands. Yo, see the holes? See My side?" (from the "Garlington Illustrated Street Version" of John 20:20). In our day, we sing about peace to the world but we don't want to *show* the peace of God to people we don't like. The problem is that Jesus topped all this off with a really difficult statement: "As the Father has sent Me, I also send you" (Jn. 20:21b).

Now that this ministry of reconciliation has been dropped into our laps, what must we do with it? *In a divided society, the Church must model unity*. Remember this answer from the previous chapter? Write it down and put it on your refrigerator, your bathroom mirror, your bedroom bureau, or any other place that you visit often. Let it sink deeply into your spirit. You are going to be tested on it! I know three reasons I can tell you this with confidence. First, this message on the ministry of reconciliation is part of God's unchanging Word. Second, He gave me a burden to preach this message all my life and to write this book for you and many others. Third, once you know to do a "right thing," then God holds you personally responsible for it. James wrote, "Therefore, to one who knows the right thing to do, and does not do it, to him it is sin" (Jas. 4:17). Prepare to be tested on your understanding and application of the ministry of reconciliation.

### How Bad Is Bad?

Given the almost unbroken string of alleged moral transgressions and hypocrisy in Congress, the White House, the Federal and state judiciaries, in abortion centers, in Hollywood, the national sports scene, and among church leaders, is there any doubt in your mind that we live in a divided society? Many Christians today seem to be waking up from a deep sleep saying, "I knew it was bad, but I didn't know how bad it actually was."

I want to talk about Jesus, the premiere minister of reconciliation. He is our model in all things. One of the things we don't realize is that when He pours His life through us, He says, "Let's get one thing positively clear: *It is going to cost you to walk with Me*. It didn't cost you to join Me, but it is going to cost you to stay with Me." And it is.

Over the years, I've observed and worked with many people who have fairly "difficult" reputations. Some I've had to deal with face to face and eye to eye. Others I've watched from the comfort of my easy chair as they have denounced other "saints and sinners" from seats of authority in Senate hearings of judicial candidates, in congressional hearings over the confirmation of presidential cabinet members, or from lofty positions of "wisdom" on national TV shows or in the White House. To tell the truth, I really wanted to hate them for their hypocritical judgments of others when their own moral failings were hanging out in public for all to see. The problem is that the Lord said to me, "Joseph, if you are going to be an authentic minister of reconciliation, then you can't count *anyone's* trespasses against him!" In other words, I don't have the luxury of reconciling people I like and despising those I don't like.

**Insincere Vacuum Salesmen**

Too many of us are like insincere vacuum cleaner salesmen. We seem to be more interested in achieving some "quota" than in listening to someone's problems. We tell people who don't know Jesus, "If you are not really interested, then tell me. I didn't come here to listen to your problems; I just want to sell you a vacuum cleaner. If you're not interested, I'm out of here." We are like that a lot of times. "You want to hear about Jesus? No? All right then, I'm out of here." We quickly dismiss unreceptive people because we don't have their best interests at heart.

I can hear the Lord saying to me, "Joseph, if you are going to reconcile the world, you will have to love the people who live in it. You can't get caught up in the fact that the enemy uses certain people because then you will start looking at the people rather than looking at the evil personality *behind* the battle. Remember that you wrestle not against flesh and blood." The reality of spiritual warfare has become vividly clear to me now. I've learned that spiritual warfare isn't just a matter of "good against evil" or "Christian against non-Christian." It also involves a war of principles, and specifically God-given principles against false principles based on fantasy, rebellion, and willfulness.

Many of the people whom we deal with from day to day haven't decided "what they want to be when they grow up" (they haven't discovered their destiny),  so they become whatever you are when they are around you. A friend of mine says these people are "chameleons on glen plaid." It's hard to be a chameleon on a checkered pattern with all kinds of colors, isn't it? Frustration is the order of the day.

## Are You "Obedience-Challenged"?

God has called us to be ministers of reconciliation to the confused and the frustrated. This isn't a call for preachers or for full-time clergy; it is a call to the entire Body of Christ. Wherever you are, *you are challenged.* I think we need a brain change. We need to change our way of thinking and understand that the highest call in the world is not to be a preacher, but *to do the will of God.* If you doubt me, just examine the life of Jesus and see what *His* emphasis was!

Whatever the will of God is for your life, that's "God's call." If God hasn't called you to be a preacher but you want to be one anyway, you will miss God's highest for your life. I know a lot of people who are trying to be preachers when they are not called to preach. People who are "obedience-challenged" are a miserable lot. I also know a lot of people who don't want to be preachers when that is what God has called them to do. The truth is that both groups of people are missing it: The highest call in the world is to *do* the will of God. The highest example of earthly obedience to a heavenly call is the life of Jesus Christ.

> *But when the fulness of the time came, God sent forth His Son, born of a woman, born under the Law, in order that He might redeem those who were under the Law, that we might receive the adoption as sons* (Galatians 4:4-5).

The Bible and secular historical sources all agree on the basics: Jesus Christ was a real person who was born in a certain time and place in history. He came into a very real family in a very real place, and His locus was ancient Israel, in what the British Empire would later call "Palestine." (The Jews have never liked this word, which was derived from the

Latin root, *Palestina*, meaning Philistine.) He was a Nazarene who was born under the Law in ancient Bethlehem, with a family lineage that could be traced in the Torah all the way back to the line of David (according to the flesh). All this can be demonstrated by history. He was born a male child, was circumcised, and was presented to the Lord in the Temple of Herod. He grew up and learned the family trade of carpentry while living with His earthly parents in perfect subjection to them until He was 30 years old. Since the heavenly Father sent Him, we can accurately say that God sent His Son in such a way that every human being on earth could identify with Him. Why?

> *But we do see Him who has been made for a little while lower than the angels, namely, Jesus, because of the suffering of death crowned with glory and honor, **that by the grace of God He might taste death for everyone**. For it was fitting for Him, for whom are all things, and through whom are all things, in bringing many sons to glory, to perfect the author of their salvation through sufferings. For both He who sanctifies and those who are sanctified are all from one Father; for which reason He is not ashamed to call them brethren, … Since then the children share in flesh and blood, He Himself likewise also partook of the same, that through death He might render powerless him who had the power of death, that is, the devil; and might deliver those who through fear of death were subject to slavery all their lives. … **Therefore, He had to be made like His brethren in all things, that He might become a merciful and faithful high priest in things pertaining to God**, to make propitiation for the sins of the people. For since **He Himself was tempted** in that which He has suffered, He is able to come to the aid of those who are tempted. Therefore, holy brethren, partakers of a heavenly calling, consider Jesus, the Apostle and High Priest of our confession. **He was faithful to Him who appointed Him**…* (Hebrews 2:9-11,14-15,17–3:2).

According to the writer of Hebrews, our High Priest, Jesus Christ, can sympathize with our weaknesses and faults and feel what we feel (see Heb. 4:14-15). The issue of race, gender, or social standing has nothing to do with the Lord's ability to feel our pain and sense of failure. He is our legitimate mediator who can totally identify with everything that we will ever go through in any way.

Our great High Priest understands gender confusion, even though we are afraid to even discuss it. He understands racism and sexism and the pain and rejection they breed. According to the inspired Word of God, our High Priest can be touched by our infirmity or feel our pain in every situation.

**Don't You Care?**

I know of two occasions in Scripture where people challenged Jesus about whether or not He sympathized with their pain. The disciples wondered whether or not Jesus cared about their fears when a violent storm threatened to swamp their boat. Jesus was sleeping in the bow at the time, but the disciples were busy hoping they wouldn't die. It must have been a terrible storm, because most of these men were expert fishermen and sailors who made their living on that same lake. The disciples got so upset that Jesus was sleeping while they "were drowning" that they shook Jesus and woke Him. Then they said, "Teacher, do You not care that we are perishing?" (Mk. 4:38). What they really said was, "Don't You care that we are drowning?"

In retrospect, it was a pretty silly question, but Jesus stood up and spoke to the wind. He didn't act ugly; He just stood and told the wind to shut up (see Mk. 4:39). He didn't say, "Now if you fools ever mess with Me and My nap again...." No, He responded to their challenge that He didn't care with a challenge of His own: "Why are you so timid? How is it that you have no faith?" (Mk. 4:40) When anyone decides to question the Lord's ability to care, He has a right to challenge their faith.

The second instance involved Martha, the religious workaholic in the Gospel of Luke. I'm being a little rough on her, but she epitomizes the way many Christians approach Jesus Christ today. Jesus had entered her house as an invited guest and Martha was agitated that He was content to continue talking with her sister, Mary, while she "slaved" in the kitchen alone (see Lk. 10:40). She was in the kitchen rattling everything she could and probably throwing the things she couldn't. She was developing a serious attitude problem. Jesus and Mary were having a great conversation as Mary sat at the Master's feet, totally ignoring Martha's temper tantrum in the next room.

Since Jesus obviously wasn't getting the message, Martha finally stormed out of the kitchen and confronted Jesus by saying, "Don't You care?" (see Lk. 10:40b). Jesus was gentle with Martha, but He made it clear that while He did care about her *feelings*, He cared about Mary's *soul* and *spiritual well-being* much more. Then He told Martha to be more like Mary (I'm sure that went over well).

### I'm Not Like You

In a Scripture passage describing the way some of God's people thought He might be overlooking their sin, the Lord completes His statement with this remarkable sentence: "These things you have done, and I kept silence; *You thought that I was just like you*; [but] I will reprove you..." (Ps. 50:21). The problem is that we think God is just like us. We expect Him to be partial, limited in understanding, or totally out of touch with our feelings and pain, but He isn't. He *can* sympathize with us in every area of life.

At times I've become angry over the deceptive maneuvers and hypocritical actions of national political or religious leaders and I felt resentment and indignation rising up. I thought God hated those men and their evil deeds as much as I did in those moments, but then He would invade my thoughts and say, "Joseph, you think I'm like you, *but I'm not*. You're not like Me, because I don't hate or resent those men—I love them."

Fresh thoughts of the Lord's loving sacrifice on the cross and God's mercy and grace flooded my mind and I began to realize that I didn't get here on my own. My goodness didn't bring me here and my righteousness didn't bring me one inch closer to God. *The only reason I am forgiven is because God had mercy on me.* In His mercy He ignored my failures and faults. He said, "Garlington is messed up, but he needs Me. He doesn't like Me, but he needs Me. He doesn't want Me, but he needs Me anyway." So He sent somebody to tell me that I needed Him and that message of hope got through. As the song "Your Grace and Mercy" states[2]:

> Your grace and mercy
> Brought me through
> I'm living this moment
> Because of You.
>
> I just want to thank You
> And praise You too
> Your grace and mercy
> Brought me through.

## Remember How You Got Here

Every now and then, we all forget how we got where we are in God's Kingdom. That is when we are tempted to set up court and throw the heaviest Bible we can find at the "offenders" of the world. "Oh God, call Your fire down from Heaven!" We have forgotten our call, but God hasn't. Don't be surprised if God shows up in your court of vengeance and says, "Child, I'm not like you. I don't even want to be like you. But I do want you to be like Me. I've called you to reconcile the world back to Me." As the Church of Jesus Christ, we need to stop saying, "America, to your knees!" We need to say, "Church, to *your* knees!" Before we can say, "Repent,

America!" we need to humble *ourselves* according to Second
Chronicles 7:14 and say, "Church, repent!" Judgment always
begins at the house of the Lord. First we must be reconciled
to God and to one another in the Body of Christ. Then and
only then can we reconcile the world to God.

We raise our voices in protest against pornography when
we have pornography pouring into our homes through
magazines and TV cable service! We are too quick to stand
back and pray, "God, I thank You that I am not like other
people," when we are actually *just like them.*

### Cost Accounting 101

Whether we like it or not, Jesus has passed along to us
His ministry of reconciliation. The plan is simple and unal-
terable. First you and I must be reconciled to God, to be
brought back to His original intent for our lives and our local churches. Then we must be reconciled to one another in
the bonds of unconditional love, "loving our neighbor as
ourselves." That is where the Church is right now.

> *Now great multitudes were going along with Him; and He
> turned and said to them, "If anyone comes to Me, and does
> not hate his own father and mother and wife and children
> and brothers and sisters* [in comparison to his love for
> Me], *yes, and even his own life, he cannot be My disciple.
> Whoever does not carry his own cross and come after Me
> cannot be My disciple. For which one of you, when he wants
> to build a tower, does not first sit down and calculate the
> cost, to see if he has enough to complete it? Otherwise, when
> he has laid a foundation, and is not able to finish, all who
> observe it begin to ridicule him, saying, 'This man began to
> build and was not able to finish'* " (Luke 14:25-30).

Jesus hasn't changed His mind. Remember, He isn't like
us. He is still telling His double-minded Church, "*It's going to
cost you to stay with Me.*" It is going to cost us our prejudice toward members of other races and social groups. It is going

to cost us our pride and lead us to publicly repent for our abuse of members of the opposite sex or our children. It will cost us our compulsive love of money, achievement, and the praise of men. It will cost us everything, and it will gain us everything. First we must be reconciled to God. Then we must be reconciled to one another. The next step is God's dream for the earth. He wants us to be ministers of reconciliation to the world, to boldly urge the lost souls around us to be reconciled to God. We need to remember that the only reason we call upon the name of the Lord today is because someone was willing to tell us the truth about God yesterday.

God's Word says that if the Church does not judge itself, He will judge it Himself:

> *For he who eats and drinks, eats and drinks judgment to himself, if he does not judge the body rightly. For this reason many among you are weak and sick, and a number sleep. But if we judged ourselves rightly, we should not be judged. But when we are judged, we are disciplined by the Lord in order that we may not be condemned along with the world* (1 Corinthians 11:29-32).

Paul says in the Book of Acts, "And the times of this ignorance God winked at; but now commandeth all men every where to repent" (Acts 17:30 KJV). I believe that God is out to capture the attention of the Church and of the world—through dramatic means if necessary. In the days ahead, I believe that we are going to see some very "significant" people in significant places dropping out of their elevated positions because God is going to "clean house." This is not the time to think that we can get away with our secret sins and hidden pleasures and still call ourselves Christians.

If you have a sin problem, then you had better take it directly to God and get that problem settled. I'm not trying to scare you. I'm simply saying that you and I live in a different season. I believe that God is going to bring judgment to national leaders and judges in America, Europe, Asia, Africa, and throughout the world, but *first* He will bring judgment to the Church. If we are wise, we will judge ourselves first and be quick to repent and be reconciled. It is time to count the cost and obey the Lord of all. He commands us to be ministers of reconciliation to a broken world, but first we must be reconciled ourselves.

### Endnote

1. *Merriam-Webster's Collegiate Dictionary*, 10th ed. (Springfield, Massachusetts: Merriam-Webster, Inc., 1994), 35-36, *ambassador*.

2. Author unknown.

# Chapter 4

# You Can't Build a House Without Tools

Did you hear about the technician who came to a manufacturing plant where a key machine in the production line wouldn't run? The plant manager said, "Man, I really need your help. We are losing a thousand dollars every half an hour that this machine is down." The technician didn't seem to be concerned about the stakes involved in the repair project. He just said, "Show me the machine." When he was brought to the site in the plant were the machine was, he said, "Turn it on." When the workers had turned it on, he listened for a few moments and then he told them, "Turn it off."

This was it. What would this technician do to bring this complex machine back on line and stem the loss of production capacity for that manufacturing plant? Every eye was on the technician as he opened his briefcase with practiced movements and took out a small ball-peen hammer. Hammer in hand, he walked over to the machine and tapped it two times. Then he said, "Turn it on again." When the shocked workmen turned on the machine, it ran perfectly. The plant manager said, "That is tremendous! How much do I owe you?"

The technician put the hammer back into his briefcase and said, "A thousand dollars." The plant manager shook his head in amazement and said, *"But it only took you two seconds!"* The technician said, "It is still a thousand dollars." The plant manager shrugged his shoulders and said, "Send me an itemized bill." A week later, the manager received an itemized bill from the technician that read:

| | |
|---|---|
| Hammer: | $ 1.00 |
| *Knowing where to hit with it*: | $ 999.00 |
| Total Due: | $1,000.00 |

If you ever hope to do something for God, you need to be equipped. One of the difficulties we face when we try to obey God is that we are often ill-equipped to do it. Any carpenter can tell you that you can't build a house without some kind of tools and knowledge. The more complex the house is, the more complex the equipment and knowledge ought to be.

How does this relate to the issue of reconciliation? In previous chapters we have said that in a divided society, the Church must model unity. The technician in our story actually walked into that manufacturing plant with two kinds of tools: the *hammer* and the *knowledge* it took to use the hammer in the right place and in the right way. We need to walk into the world equipped with God's tools and the wisdom and knowledge to use them properly. Our master model for this is Jesus Christ, the first minister of reconciliation God sent into the world. Look closely at two Scripture passages about Him, the first from the Old Testament and the second from the New Testament.

*Then a shoot will spring from the stem of Jesse, and a branch from his roots will bear fruit. And the **Spirit of the***

*Lord will rest on Him, the spirit of **wisdom** and **under-standing**, the spirit of **counsel** and **strength**, the spirit of **knowledge** and **the fear of the Lord**. And He will delight in the fear of the Lord, and He will not judge by what His eyes see, nor make a decision by what His ears hear; but with righteousness He will judge the poor, and decide with fairness for the afflicted of the earth; and He will strike the earth with the rod of His mouth, and with the breath of His lips He will slay the wicked. Also righteousness will be the belt about His loins, and faithfulness the belt about His waist* (Isaiah 11:1-5).

*And around the throne were twenty-four thrones; and upon the thrones I saw twenty-four elders sitting, clothed in white garments, and golden crowns on their heads. And from the throne proceed flashes of lightning and sounds and peals of thunder. And there were **seven lamps of fire burning** before the throne, **which are the seven Spirits of God*** (Revelation 4:4-5).

John the Revelator is not suggesting that God has seven spirits. A better translation might be "the *sevenfold* Spirit of God." There is an uncanny resemblance here to the seven "spirits" outlined by the prophet Isaiah. He mentions the *Spirit of the Lord* (the lordship of Jehovah, the eternally existent One), which is expanded in his references to Christ as the "rod" from the stem of Jesse. The rod is a traditional symbol of rulership and authority. Second, Isaiah mentions the *spirit of wisdom*; third, the *spirit of understanding*; fourth, the *spirit of counsel*; fifth, the *spirit of strength*; sixth, the *spirit of knowledge*; and seventh, the *spirit of the fear of the Lord*. This is a prophetic picture of the sevenfold Spirit of God that would operate through the ministry and presence of the Lord Jesus Christ when He would come to dwell among men centuries later.

Isaiah attributed this sevenfold Spirit of God to Jesus, the first minister of reconciliation sent to the earth. That job—

and the authority to accomplish it—has been passed on to you and me as part of the Church, and *we can do no less than He did*. Have you ever heard the expression, "I can't hear what you're saying for seeing what you are doing"? It was coined to describe a blatant contradiction between a person's words and actions (the Bible calls it *hypocrisy*). Jesus expected our words to perfectly match our actions as His did. Paul said, "Be imitators of me, just as I also am of Christ" (1 Cor. 11:1).

Reconciliation occurs in an environment of love, not judgment. I remember hearing the late John Wimber say on one occasion, "You can pray for thousands of people and there will be a number of them who won't be healed. But there shouldn't be anyone that you pray for who goes away not knowing that God loves them." If we have the power, authority, and gifting to communicate anything at all, we can reassure them that God loves them. We don't have to tell the world about judgment; they already know about it according to the writer of Hebrews:

> *For if we go on sinning willfully after receiving the knowledge of the truth, there no longer remains a sacrifice for sins, but* **a certain terrifying expectation of judgment,** *and* THE FURY OF A FIRE WHICH WILL CONSUME THE ADVERSARIES (Hebrews 10:26-27).

Have you ever thought about what life is like when you know you ought to be doing the right thing and aren't? (If you're like me, then you have probably experienced this firsthand.) When unpleasant consequences happen in your life, you kind of expect it ahead of time. If your finances suddenly collapse around your head, the chances are that your first thought will be, "Well, I guess it is because I haven't tithed." It's like the man who went to the doctor and was asked, "What have you been eating?" He said, "Well, a little bit of this and a little bit of that." The doctor said, "Well, all of those little bits must have had a lot of fat in them then.

Your cholesterol is about 300!" The man didn't act surprised at all, and his reply tells us why: "I kind of figured that was what you were going to say, Doc."

People who are not walking with God have a certain fearful expectation of judgment, so the last thing they need to hear from us is, "Judgment is coming. Turn or burn, sucker!" They already know that; they need to know there is an alternative. The problem is that too many Christians are more interested in offering them judgment, the very thing that they fear. We want to say, "God, don't let anybody in who doesn't like our message." Our prayer really ought to be, "God, don't let me be such an abrasive model of what the Kingdom of God is, because nobody will like Your message if they think You are like me."

## The Spirit of the Lord (Jehovah)

Isaiah's wonderful picture of the Lord says, "And the Spirit of the Lord will rest on Him" (Is. 11:2a). Compare it with Paul's statement: "...where the Spirit of the Lord is, there is liberty" (2 Cor. 3:17). Let's paraphrase this expansion and say it this way: "Where the Spirit of the Lord and of His Lordship is, there is genuine liberty." Another way of saying it is this: "Where Jesus is Lord, there will always be freedom." When someone asks, "Have you brought your life under the lordship of Jesus Christ?" what is the first thing you think about? We don't think about what we've gained; we think about what Jesus is going to ask us to give up! We usually don't think of the lordship of Jesus Christ as something that is wonderfully liberating. Why? I think it's because the English word *lord* is more or less synonymous with the word *dictator*.

Now if you ever want to see someone who was absolutely free, look at Jesus! Jesus was totally submitted to His Father, but at the same time He was totally free. What was His life like? He completely impacted our world. Even unconverted people quote His statements, and millions are moved by Him and pray to Him every day. He lived His life according to one simple guideline: "*I only do the things that please the Father*" (see Jn. 8:28). If we totally surrender to God, His eternal Spirit engulfs us with His glory and power. In the eyes of others (including the enemy), we take on the appearance, power, and eternal authority of our Master, the One we love. At times the enemy wonders whether he is dealing with a redeemed son of Adam or Jehovah Himself because the pain he feels from God's presence is the same!

Unfortunately, few of us ever surrender our lives totally to God, so there is no place or throne in our lives in which the Spirit of the Lord (or Jehovah) may settle down. Most of us have the sneaking suspicion that once we really surrender our life to the Lord, then He is going to "mess it up." That is because the enemy has sown doubts in our hearts about the goodness of God. This is the same trick satan pulled on Eve in the Garden of Eden. There are no new tricks in satan's bag, but that doesn't seem to cramp his style because we keep falling for his same old tricks generation after generation. All the devil does is dress up his snare a little bit differently, or ask the same old question a different way, but it always amounts to this, "Did God *really* say this?"

Isaiah's prophecy about Jesus (and those who would follow Him) seems to describe seven spirits, but he really names the one Spirit (of Jehovah), and the six manifestations of that Spirit that follow seem to be expansions of attributes of the Lord Himself. These spirits or attributes of Jehovah are grouped in pairs because they tend to work together and balance one another as well.

### The Spirit of Wisdom and Understanding

Even if you had all the information in the world, if you couldn't use it to get yourself out of a ditch, it would not be worth much to you. Isaiah described wisdom this way: "The

Lord God hath given me the tongue of the learned, that I should know how to speak a word in season to him that is weary..." (Is. 50:4a KJV). Paul talks about "the word of wisdom" and "the word of knowledge" in First Corinthians 12:8 as gifts that the Holy Spirit gives to believers for the benefit of the Church and to help us obey God's commands. This sounds very similar to some of the seven "spirits" mentioned by Isaiah that were continually manifested in Jesus' life. Why? Because this sevenfold Spirit of God is the Holy Spirit—and He will do the same in your life if you totally yield to God.

We need wisdom, and it only comes as we are reconciled with God. Wisdom doesn't come from man's books, universities, or philosophies. It only comes from God. One dictionary definition of a person who is wise is that he is "characterized by wisdom: marked by deep understanding, keen discernment, and a capacity for sound judgment...evidencing or hinting at the possession of inside information."[1]

### The Spirit of Counsel and Might

Isaiah also linked together the spirit of counsel with the spirit of might. At first this combination seemed odd to me, but then I looked at the original Hebrew words used by the prophet. In God's realm, "counsel" (*'etsah* in Hebrew) means "plan, prudence, and purpose."[2] Jesus had a spirit of divine purpose, a holy counsel about Him. He was pursuing His Father's divine plan with a supernatural strength and power. The word for "might," *gebuwrah*, literally means "force, mastery, mighty power, strength," as the things that create champions and chief warriors.[3] The *spirit of force and mastery* works to accomplish the things laid out by the *spirit of counsel or divine purpose*. Counsel and might are linked together by God for a divine reason.

### The Spirit of Knowledge and the Fear of the Lord

Why would the spirit of knowledge be linked with the fear or awe of the Lord? The apostle Paul knew the answer.

He warns us, "*Knowledge makes arrogant*, but love edifies. If anyone supposes that he knows anything, he has not yet known as he ought to know" (1 Cor. 8:1b-2).

Have you ever noticed that God will give you information in one minute that you just didn't have access to moments before? If every problem or conflict in our lives could be dealt with using our own intelligence and abilities, then we wouldn't need God. It's obvious that we *desperately* need God, so we also need His knowledge. But this knowledge should always be mixed with reverent awe of God, and this reverence or "fear" of God is a natural part of being reconciled to Him. The Scriptures say:

> *The fear of the Lord is clean, enduring forever; the judgments of the Lord are true; they are righteous altogether. They are more desirable than gold, yes, than much fine gold; sweeter also than honey and the drippings of the honeycomb. Moreover, by them Thy servant is warned; in keeping them there is great reward* (Psalm 19:9-11).

I believe that when you understand the fear of God you understand something about awe and wonder and the ultimate issues of life. This has nothing to do with a fear that we will "lose our salvation." Rather, it refers to a healthy awe and respect of the Almighty God whom we serve. We stand in His shadow, not our own strength.

## Four Examples of the Sevenfold Spirit at Work

The "sevenfold Spirit of God" is really the Holy Spirit, and it is impossible to subdivide the ways He works in our lives to reconcile us to God and to other people.

I remember a brother who was constantly listening to hear what God had to say in every situation. He found himself aboard a ship where the crew was having a difficult time restarting a massive rotor in the engine room. After the crewmen had struggled and agonized over the problem to the point of frustration, they called in this man. He showed up and looked at this thing and said, "Did you try such and such?" They said, "No, we haven't." When they tried the procedure he recommended, the rotor instantly began to rotate the way it was made to operate.

The astounded crew members looked at the engineer and said, "How did you do that?" He said, "Let's have a cup of coffee." When they were all seated around a table with their coffee, my friend told them, "Right after I got your call, I prayed and asked God, 'Tell me what the problem is.' And He did!" He was careful to give God the glory for the supernatural knowledge, wisdom, and understanding he received by the Spirit of God. As usual, these insights were imparted to create an opportunity for this man to share the reality of God with people who didn't know Him.

God has a way of bypassing all the man-made ways of solving problems at times just to remind us that He is God (and we aren't). When we give ourselves to the Lord, He releases in us wisdom to apply the information we have under certain circumstances. If we are not taking advantage of that heavenly resource, then we are missing a tremendous flow of God's life through us. He wants to be a part of what you do on your job, in your house, in your marriage, and in your local church. It is true that nothing is too hard for God, but it is also true that nothing is beneath Him either.

I'm convinced that if we will open our hearts to the Holy Spirit, we will find supernatural things happening through us by accident. In those times when the Holy Spirit shows you things, you need to respond to what He shows you. Remember that the spirit of wisdom doesn't operate with your wisdom; it operates with God's wisdom.

### Does "Imbecile" Mean Anything to You?

One time I was with a group of people who were asked to pray for a man. We prayed, "Oh God, help us to know how to pray for this man." Then I saw a stereotypical picture of a really imbecilic-looking face. I kept looking at that face and wondering, *What is that?* The Holy Spirit spoke to my heart and said, "It's an imbecile." I said, "Oh yeah, that's what that is. It's an imbecile." I had been given knowledge of a secret thing by God, but now I needed the wisdom to know what to do with it. How could I tell the man whom we were praying for, "Brother, when I was praying for you I saw this picture of an imbecile"?

I needed wisdom at that point and that's what I asked the Holy Spirit to give me. I felt prompted to ask the man, "Does the word *imbecile* mean anything to you?" He said no, and I thought to myself, *I guess I missed it. I'll never do this again. This is the last time You sucker me into that, Lord.* A few minutes later the man asked me, "Can I say something to you about the word *imbecile?*" I said, "Sure." Then he told me, "My dad used to call me an imbecile every day of my life. If I did something wrong, it was 'Imbecile!' "

Now I didn't know that, but God knew that. Armed with knowledge, wisdom, and guidance on how to pray, our team began to pray with this precious man of God and set him free from this painful memory of his past. In that prayer, we became agents of reconciliation because he needed to be reconciled to his father. I'm glad to report that God wonderfully touched him.

I was in Atlanta preaching on the subject of faith and our need to step out in daring obedience to God despite the risks, but this time (one of the rare times in my ministry), my message was somehow completed in only 20 minutes. I didn't have any jokes, illustrations, or extra comments left to fill the time either, and the service wasn't even half over! So there I was standing right there in front of everybody, breathing the prayer, "Lord, what are we up to?" He replied, "Whatever you want to do, son. This time I'm going to do whatever you want to do. Whatever you do, I am going to be with you."

## Why Did I Say That?

Now this sounded like a pretty risky proposition to me because I didn't want to risk Him saying, "Garlington, that is the dumbest thing I ever heard. I've changed My mind—I'm not going to be a part of that thing at all!" So I said, "God, I don't want to miss You." Once again He seemed to say to my heart, "Whatever you want to do, I'm going to be with you." Finally I said, "Okay, God." In that moment, the question popped into my mind and came right out of my mouth (and over the sound system to the congregation): "Is there anybody here with scoliosis?" It just came right out of my mouth, and I thought, *Why did I say that? I don't even know what scoliosis is!*

I had heard the word used in reference to diseases in several places of the body, but I just couldn't remember what it was. Then a lady stood up and came right down the aisle and stood in front of me, expecting me to lay hands on her and pray. Meanwhile I was praying silently, *God, I don't even know where to put my hands to pray for scoliosis.* Then a solution occurred to me that I sensed was a product or fruit of the Spirit of wisdom at work in me. I asked the lady, "Would you stand here please? Now turn around and tell the audience what 'scoliosis' is." If she had said, "I don't know," then we would have been in real trouble. God healed her along with a number of other people who needed His healing touch. In retrospect I could see that God had cut my message short so He could get on about the business of taking care of His people.

## "Hey Buddy, Your Sin Is Showing"

Let me give you another illustration from the ministry of the late John Wimber. I once heard him share a story of an experience he had after boarding a plane, when he was "just minding his own business." As he walked toward one of the passengers sitting in an aisle seat, he saw the letters, A-D-U-L-T-E-R-E-R, written right across the man's forehead just as clearly as if someone had written it with a large black felt-tip marker! He couldn't help but stare at the letters, and the man in the aisle seat wasn't amused. He glared right back at him and said, "Do you know me? Why are you looking at me like that?" This jarred John out of his staring spell. He shook his head and was relieved to see that the letters were gone.

Naturally, when he looked down at his ticket, he discovered that he had been assigned the seat right beside the man with the "graffiti forehead." So he sat down and did his best to shake off his eerie experience, but as soon as he looked at the man beside him, he saw the word *ADULTERER* spelled out across his forehead. John quickly turned away and then looked back again. The letters were still there—A-D-U-L-T-E-R-E-R—emblazoned on his forehead. John must have been staring and squinting his eyes pretty hard in his efforts to make the word go away because the guy finally decided that he had had enough. He asked John Wimber, "What is the matter? Why are you staring at me?" John turned to this man and said in a soft voice that only the passenger could hear, "I don't know how to say this to you any other way, so I'm just going to say it: *As I was coming to my seat, I saw the word 'ADULTERER' written across your forehead.*"

The moment the words were spoken, this man turned pale. As soon as the plane had taken off and reached cruising altitude, the man leaned over and asked John, "Can I talk to you?" John quickly said, "Sure," and the man asked, "Can we go upstairs?" (This incident took place on a Boeing 747 jetliner, which has a refreshment bar on a second level. Apparently, the man's wife had been sitting next to him. This is the reason he had wanted to go upstairs to talk.)

This man opened his heart to John Wimber, explaining that he had been having an affair and going into all the details of his disintegrating life. While the man was talking, God gave John some more insight into what was going on in this man's life. Right there cruising at 35,000 feet, he shared the good news of Jesus Christ with the man while standing at the bar in a Boeing 747. Not only was the man weeping, but the flight attendant serving them at the bar was weeping too! The man looked up in his tears and interrupted John to say, "Can you hold it a minute? I want to go downstairs and get my wife." He went downstairs and told his wife what was going on and she agreed to come upstairs too. Then John was able to lead both the husband and his wife to the Lord. This is just one example of what happens when we are open to the supernatural and to the dynamic power that God makes available to us when we commit ourselves to the message and ministry of reconciliation.

If you look through the New Testament, you will not find a single broken person who ever came to Jesus and didn't receive some kind of uplifting, healing, or instructive word from Him. Why? Because Jesus Christ was—and is—in the business of reconciling people to God. It's about time for us to catch on to that too. Sinners never received a judgment message from Jesus; He reserved that for religious hypocrites who were into judgmentalism.

Every day, Jesus made it a point to minister to people who were hungry for God and eager to receive mercy, forgiveness, and healing. Meanwhile the religious people of His day were constantly saying, "If He only knew what kind of persons these people are...." They weren't interested in reconciliation; they were after retribution, judgment, and punishment for wrongdoers. (Sounds like some of us in the modern Church, doesn't it?)

Let me summarize and end with a question: What did Jesus pass on to us? A ministry of reconciliation with a message of love or a ministry of judgment with a message of mercilessness and destruction? (What does your life as a follower of Jesus say about your choice between these two ministries?)

## Endnotes

1. *Merriam-Webster's Collegiate Dictionary*, 10th ed., (Springfield, Massachusetts: Merriam-Webster, Inc., 1994), 1358, *wise*.

2. James Strong, *Strong's Exhaustive Concordance of the Bible* (Peabody, Massachusetts: Hendrickson Publishers, n.d.), *counsel* (H6098). (These meanings are drawn from their prime root words and so may not be exact to *Strong's*.)

3. *Strong's*, *might* (H1369, H1368).

# Chapter 5

# Forget Your Dignity— Get Hold of God!

There was a church that suddenly began to experience a tremendous move of the Holy Spirit. Every time an altar call was given, people would rush to the altar to repent of their sins, and people were getting saved in every service. This whirlwind of anointing just seemed to come out of nowhere, and nobody could figure out what was taking place. (If you are aware of what God is doing in renewal and revival around the world as of this writing, then this should sound very familiar to you.) One night the pastor's wife awoke from a sound sleep and noticed that her husband was not in the bed, and she became concerned.

She put on her robe and walked through the house looking in every room for him, with no success. Her concern was growing, and she even walked downstairs to check the basement, but couldn't find him there. Then she heard a noise out in the garage. She carefully opened the door to see what or who had made the sound. It was her husband. It almost broke her heart to see him huddled up in a blanket, leaning against the rear tire of their car, just crying his eyes out like a heartbroken child. He was totally oblivious to her presence as he poured out his spirit in intercessory prayer, saying, "Give me souls, Lord! Give me souls...."

The pastor's wife quietly closed the door to the garage and walked away from that encounter knowing without a doubt that she had uncovered the true source of the white-hot revival and harvest of souls in the church.

The devil's schemes to destroy and enslave mankind don't get broken on the street. We can pass out all the tracts that we want to, or enroll in a lifetime of self-improvement courses. We can demonstrate until we wear out our shoes and our welcome, and that's okay to do, but we must *never* think that our outward acts alone can bring change in the realm of men and angels. It is impossible to accomplish the works of God through the flesh alone. As God warned Zerubbabel long ago, it is "...not by might nor by power, but by My Spirit" (Zech. 4:6). The apostle Paul told the Corinthian believers:

> *And when I came to you, brethren, I did not come with superiority of speech or of wisdom, proclaiming to you the testimony of God. For I determined to know nothing among you except Jesus Christ, and Him crucified. And I was with you in weakness and in fear and in much trembling. And my message and my preaching were not in persuasive words of wisdom, but in demonstration of the Spirit and of power, that your faith should not rest on the wisdom of men, but on the power of God* (1 Corinthians 2:1-5).

Paul the apostle had the training and the intellectual tools to hold his own among the Epicurean and Stoic philosophers of Greece in the Athenian Areopagus (or "Mars Hill"), but he didn't rely on his natural talents or abilities. He told the Corinthian believers that the true strength of his ministry was rooted "in demonstration of the Spirit and of power" (1 Cor. 2:4b). Can we say the same today?

*If our faith is going to rest anywhere, it's got to rest in the power of God.* Even though the names have changed, we are still battling against "...the rulers, against the powers, against the world forces of this darkness, against the spiritual forces of wickedness in the heavenly places" (Eph. 6:12). It is only when we pull them down from "up there" in the heavenlies that something gets pulled down "down here" in the earth where they affect the human race. Jesus couldn't have made it any clearer (but it is still slow to soak into our brains) when He said:

*Truly I say to you, whatever you shall bind on earth shall be bound in heaven; and whatever you loose on earth shall be loosed in heaven. Again I say to you, that if two of you agree on earth about anything that they may ask, it shall be done for them **by My Father** who is in heaven. For where two or three have gathered together in My name, **there I am** in their midst* (Matthew 18:18-20).

Change on the earthly level often requires travail or hard work in prayer that produces change in the spirit realm first. Before Jesus began a day full of miracles and anointed ministry, He spent hours and even entire nights in prayer laying a groundwork of the miraculous in prayer *first*. The disciples were surprised when a demon refused to yield to their shouted commands to come out, and Jesus had to come and personally deliver a boy from demonic possession and save the embarrassed disciples from an angry crowd.

What He told them should be a warning to anyone who intends to enter the spiritual battle for souls and reconciliation:

*And He said to them, "Because of the littleness of your faith; for truly I say to you, if you have faith as a mustard seed, you shall say to this mountain, 'Move from here to there,' and it shall move; and nothing shall be impossible to you. [But this kind does not go out except by prayer and fasting]"* (Matthew 17:20-21).

If something isn't bound "up there," then don't expect it to be bound "down here." If an evil force isn't bound in the heavenlies, then it's not going to be bound in the Supreme Court or the chamber rooms of Congress. If it isn't bound above, then it won't be bound in the examination rooms of the abortion clinic downtown. We need to learn something about *travail*, a word usually associated with the natural birth process. (Men are especially ignorant in this area, and for obvious reasons.) The most important thing you have to learn is that certain things don't "come" just because you want them to. Some things won't happen just because you formed a focus group or set up a lobbying organization.

Daniel discovered that his prayers triggered a heavenly battle between the Archangel Michael and the demonic prince of Persia, and that the conflict would later spread to include the demonic prince over Greece! Today our prayers might trigger a battle between Heaven's hosts and the demonic prince over Pittsburgh, Denver, or Sacramento. Regardless of which demonic prince you are dealing with, you don't come against them arrogantly. You humble yourself under the mighty hand of God and let Him exalt you in due time (see 1 Pet. 5:6).

The same principle holds true when you are confronting the demonic source fueling the fires of racism, violence, suicide, drug addiction, or sexual abuse. You humble yourself under the mighty hand of God and go to war in the heavenlies fully aware that if the battle is going to be won, it will be won by *God alone* acting on your behalf in response to your godly, humble prayer! That is a mouthful, but it is the key to victory in every area of spiritual warfare.

The volume of our shouts doesn't faze the enemy, although *if God tells you to shout*, then you had better shout! It is the *obedience* of your prayers that yields results. Daniel was innocent of the sins his nation had committed, but he honored God by standing in the gap and taking the sin of his nation upon his own shoulders. This is the heart of intercessory prayer. It is the mark of Christ-like prayer, of redemptive prayer, of reformation prayer. It is this kind of prayer that demolishes strongholds and transforms entire nations. We just need to remind ourselves that it is God who will tread down the enemy. It is God who is going to do it.

**Slow, Slower, and Stop**

One of the hardest things about spiritual warfare through prayer is the "time thing." God is not in a hurry like we are. That is why He tells us things like, "For the vision is yet for the appointed time; it hastens toward the goal, and it will not fail. Though it tarries, wait for it; for it will certainly come, it will not delay" (Hab. 2:3). God seems to have three speeds: slow, slower, and stop. That's it. If you get upset with Him, He stops walking altogether because He won't go anywhere or do anything to bless a bad attitude. Look closely at the principle God gave when He said through Paul, "...we are ready to punish all disobedience, *whenever your obedience is complete*" (2 Cor. 10:6).

In a single sentence, God can describe your problem, help you understand what it is and why it is troubling you, and deliver complete supernatural healing to your area of hurt. On the other hand, you can sit in a counseling session with the nation's top experts or attend expensive "self-help" seminars for hours, weeks, or even months and never get your problems solved. The key is moving yourself into the presence of God. Too many of us are all too quick to say, "Will you pray for me?" God wants us to start saying, "No, pray for yourself." Yes, we ought to pray for one another, but we should never allow it to displace the necessity for individuals to get hold of God themselves.

There is something about desperate need or boldfaced determination to touch God that just doesn't care about dignity or appearances. The woman with the issue of blood thought to herself, *If I could just touch the hem of Jesus' garment...*

(see Mk. 5:25-34). She had already seen all the doctors she could afford to see. She had exhausted every earthly resource, and her future looked dim. Now that she saw hope walking right past her, she wasn't looking around for a friendly face to ask, "Would you get Jesus' attention for me?" She couldn't care less if somebody got offended and said, "Hey, lady, you've gotta wait your turn. Get in line like the rest of us—we all want to get healed." She only had a little strength left, and she had everything to gain and nothing to lose.

That frail woman was just a little more desperate than the mob of people packed in around Jesus. Somehow she shoved, pushed, and crawled her way right through that crushing mass of humanity to touch the hem of Jesus' garment (she had to have been at ground level because the hem was at the bottom) and was instantly healed! Somehow I doubt if this woman's hair was in place when she finally stood up. Her clothing was probably torn and her hands, knees, and face were probably covered in dust from crawling on the ground. She didn't look like she had much dignity at the end, but it didn't matter. She had touched Jesus and she was totally healed and set free! Who needs dignity when you've just been delivered from death's door and set free by the Messiah!? We have got to understand what is really important if we want to touch Jesus.

### Forget Your Dignity

If you are determined to get hold of God, then you can't afford to be concerned when other people think your unconventional or eager path to Jesus isn't very "couth." So what? Get deliverance *first* (whether it's for yourself or someone else). Forget your dignity. You can always get your dignity later!

*The weapons we fight with are not the weapons of the world. On the contrary, they have divine power to demolish*

> ***strongholds***. *We demolish **arguments** and every **pretension** that sets itself up against the knowledge of God, and we take captive every thought to make it obedient to Christ* (2 Corinthians 10:4-5 NIV).

God calls us to prayer when He calls us to the ministry of reconciliation. He also gives us extremely powerful weapons to help us do our job in the earth. What do we do with these weapons? They have divine power to demolish strongholds. Strongholds are the things in which people trust. According to Proverbs 21:22, "A wise man scales the city of the mighty, and brings down the stronghold in which they trust." Now how do we pull down strongholds? We use the divinely powerful weapons God has given us, and wisdom is one of them, according to this verse. You don't just go jumping on strongholds by yourself either. The stronger the demonic force is, the more you need to rally the troops together and say, "It's going to take all of us praying in agreement and unity. One will chase 1,000; two will put 10,000 to flight, and a threefold cord is not quickly broken" (see Deut. 32:30; Eccles. 4:12).

You're always on good ground when you have three people agreeing about something. The tough part is getting three to agree. Jesus said, "For where two or three have gathered together in My name, there I am in their midst" (see Mt. 18:20). I remember Bob Mumford remarking to me—with tongue firmly planted in his cheek—that this passage should read, "If two or three of you *ever* get together, I'll come to see it Myself!"

Another part of our call to reconciliation involves tearing down ancient strongholds like racism, religious prejudice, ethnic and economic conflicts, etc. This means our call won't always be pleasant or easy, but as the line goes in the movie, *The Blues Brothers*, "We are on a mission from God." However, when you are looking at something that could bring you face-to-face with racial or political hostilities that have gone on for centuries, you have to ask the question, "Who in his right mind would do this?" This is not a "high five" moment. It isn't a time to say, "Yeah, brothers!" This is the time to walk in a real sense of humility because every step that you take in the Kingdom, every inch of Kingdom ground, is contested soil. If you decide to do something that God has called you to do, you are going to be contested in that decision. That is why the first posture we should take in doing the will of God is the one Peter advised:

> *Humble yourselves, therefore, under the mighty hand of God, that He may exalt you at the proper time, casting all your anxiety upon Him, because He cares for you* (1 Peter 5:6-7).

Now if you don't humble yourself, you will find yourself facing a fallen angelic foe all alone because God doesn't back braggers. "Hey, we can do this. Last night we took on the whole kingdom of darkness and we stuck it in their face." That isn't the Kingdom attitude. We should be saying, "God, You were gracious to us and we are grateful to You. You were merciful and we appreciate Your standing with us." When we begin to appreciate the awesomeness of these tasks, we will say, like Paul the apostle, "Who is sufficient for these things?" (2 Cor. 2:16b KJV) The answer to the question is simply this: *Christ is our sufficiency.*

### All-Star Dribbler

A friend of mine was ministering one night with a special anointing that was simply amazing. It was the first of three nights that he was scheduled to speak, and everything went right that night. The special music was exceptional, the choir was wonderful, and my friend preached one of the best messages he had ever preached in his life. On the way home he said to himself, *Man, that was the real you tonight. That was the real you.*

On the second night, he was scheduled to speak again, and he looked forward to a repeat performance. But this time, the special music wasn't like it should have been, the choir wasn't up to snuff, and as for my friend's message, he later told me, "My sermon dribbled off of my lip, down my shirt, and onto the floor." On his way home, my friend asked, "Lord, what happened tonight?" The Lord said, *"Last night was Me. Tonight was you."*

> *Abide in Me, and I in you. As the branch cannot bear fruit of itself, unless it abides in the vine, so neither can you, unless you abide in Me. I am the vine, you are the branches; he who abides in Me, and I in him, he bears much fruit; for* **apart from Me you can do nothing** (John 15:4-5).

You can't bear fruit apart from the Lord, so whatever is going on, if the initiative is not His, then the fruit won't be His. If the initiative is His, then the fruit will be His if we do it His way. God is calling us to a clear understanding of this eternal principle. No matter how many prophetic mandates (and I do believe in them) you receive, no matter the glowing words of encouragement or exhortation that people say to you, make sure you place them squarely *behind* the direct warning of Jesus Christ: "Apart from Me you can do nothing." That goes for you and me, for the Church, for the pastor down the street at "First Church," and for the most educated theologian and most talented musician on the planet. Apart from the Lord, we can do nothing.

Our weapons are not worldly weapons. The ultimate job can be done only by the power of the Holy Spirit. Our warfare is not political, physical, or even philosophical in nature, although it affects all these areas; it is spiritual warfare. Our enemies are spiritual enemies. We wrestle not against flesh and blood. This means that when we meet racists, no matter what color the racists are, those racists are not the enemy—it is the evil spirit motivating their racist behavior. You are not going to pull down strongholds until you deal with the spiritual thing upholding them. When you remove the foundations, then the stuff that's held together by demonic spiritual rule—like the arguments and pretentions—will begin to fall apart like a house of cards.

The Old Testament record describes cosmic battles leading to the demolition of ancient kingdoms and dynasties such as Babylon in apocalyptic terms, describing conflicts that cause "the stars to fall to the earth." The most dramatic of these references concerns the fall of lucifer the archangel and a third of the angels of Heaven (see Is. 14:4-17; Lk. 10:18; Rev. 9:1). The Book of Revelation describes satan as a great dragon whose "...tail swept away *a third of the stars* of heaven, and threw them to the earth" (Rev. 12:4a). Obviously these stars were angelic beings who chose to walk in rebellion with satan. Literal stars were not falling from Heaven; these were spiritual spheres of power, influence, and authority.

The conflict between the angels of Heaven and demonic princes is perfectly pictured in the Book of Daniel when two angelic princes from Heaven were dispatched in answer to Daniel's intercession over a 21-day period. Daniel's part was to pray and stand firmly in determination. It was *not* his part to personally do combat with satan or one of his stooges. There is a good reason for that. This being who appeared to Daniel wasn't some muscle-bound earthly warrior. Look at what his appearance alone did to Daniel, the man who personally faced down kings and death itself:

> *His body also was like beryl, his face had the appearance of lightning, his eyes were like flaming torches, his arms and feet like the gleam of polished bronze, and the sound of his words like the sound of a tumult. Now I, Daniel, alone saw the vision, while the men who were with me did not see the vision; nevertheless, a great dread fell on them, and they ran away to hide themselves. So I was left alone and saw this great vision; yet no strength was left in me, for my natural*

*color turned to a deathly pallor, and I retained no strength* (Daniel 10:6-8).

This powerful angel explained that Daniel's prayer was *heard and answered* 21 days earlier, the very moment he prayed it. So was the mail slow? Did the delivery company go on strike? No, this powerful angel told Daniel that he had been fought to a standstill by the powerful fallen angel or prince over Persia—the very country in which Daniel was living as a prisoner in the king's palace. Evidently God had had enough and He then dispatched His "Terminator" to the scene. "But the prince of the kingdom of Persia was withstanding me for twenty-one days; then behold, *Michael, one of the chief princes*, came to help me, for I had been left there with the kings of Persia" (Dan. 10:13).

Every kingdom—even democracies, bureaucracies, and autocracies—has principalities. Things are changed on earth by changing the balance of power in the heavenly realm of principalities, powers, and rulers. If we don't understand that we are dealing with spiritual realities, then we will get stuck somewhere standing in front of a courthouse with petitions or circling an abortion clinic with placards to no avail. The ungodly activities will go on untroubled and untouched by our earthbound effort.

You can't change racism with a petition, unless it's a *prayer petition* that continually goes up before God. You can moderate, you can modify, you can multiply, and sometimes you can even make some temporary improvements in a situation, but you cannot make radical root changes apart from the Spirit of God. The wisest course is to change the status of it in the heavenlies first, and *then* follow through with grassroots actions on earth. That is the modern equivalent of David seeking God about an invading force, receiving assurance that God has won the battle, and then going out to "mop up" behind God's angelic armies.

Daniel's fervent prayer for his nation is an example that we need to notice and imitate. Our second but greatest example of someone who "got hold of God" on behalf of others is Jesus. Daniel and Jesus both used fervent prayer and fasting to transcend the affairs and constant crises of earth, and they both upended the political and religious powers of their day in accordance with God's will. Both of them specifically humbled themselves before God the Father, and they both took upon themselves the sins of others (Jesus to a much greater extent of course).

So when we finally decide to get about our Father's business, we need to move in the dimension of the Spirit where the real changes can take place. You will never see it printed in the secular press, but the real force that brought down the "Iron Curtain" dividing Eastern Europe was the angelic force released in answer to the prayers and petitions of faithful believers who fervently bombarded Heaven over the years. The West was shocked to see so many strong Christian voices in those former Communist nations rise up and talk about Jesus when the Berlin Wall came down. At the same time, people had long forgotten the defiant words of the late Nikita Khrushchev, the premier of the former Soviet Union who pounded his shoe on his desk in the general assembly of the United Nations in the 1960's and scared a whole generation of Americans silly when he shouted, "We will bury you."

Not many Americans today know who this man was, but it appears that Communism in that part of the world is no longer an "ism"; it's a "wasm." This could quickly change if Christians fail to stay alert in prayer. The demonic prince behind the plague of communism can quickly raise up his ugly head again. The weapons of our warfare are not worldly. They are not carnal weapons.

Some years ago, the Holy Spirit would wake me up every night almost like clockwork, at 12:30 or 1:00 a.m. He would say, "Go pray. Intercede." One night I was on my hands and knees in fervent prayer when all of a sudden I sensed a "violence" in my spirit. A righteous indignation rose up in me and I heard the phrase, "Break it," rise up in me. So I laid aside my pride and began to pound on the floor and say, "Break it! Break it!" I didn't know what was going on, but I obeyed the Lord anyway. I kept saying (and shouting), "Break it! Break it!" and pounding the floor for 15 minutes, and then I fell off to sleep right there on the floor.

What happened next is very important: While I was sleeping I had a dream. In my dream I was in a room that had been fitted with a suspended ceiling. But I noticed that instead of using wires to hang the ceiling framework from the roof joists, 2-inch by 2-inch boards had been used, which is very unusual. This indicated to me the mass or heaviness of the ceiling material. As I walked around in the room, I could see great gaping holes in the ceiling. In fact, there were some places where I could see past the suspended ceiling all the way up into the roof and beyond! I said, "God, what is this?" He said, "That is what you have been breaking." God was helping me to see something that was taking place in the spiritual dimension, even though I didn't understand it right away.

The following Sunday, our church congregation experienced a phenomenal breakthrough in the Holy Spirit as if the heavens were opened wide right over us. I immediately understood what the Lord was telling me. He had prompted me to break up the barriers between us and Heaven through aggressive and authoritative intercessory prayer, and the fruits of that spiritual victory manifested themselves as victory among God's people on the earth.

Most of the divisions in the Church and in society stem from "aberrations," from wrongs and from sin committed in the past and in the present. Most if not all of these were prompted or staged by demonic forces in the heavenlies, much as Adam and Eve's sin in the Garden was preceded by carefully designed temptation and persuasion by satan, the tempter. As ministers of reconciliation, we are called to deal with the aberrations wherever we find them, but *not in the flesh*. We battle in prayer in the heavenlies, and in love on earth.

Our challenge as ministers of reconciliation is to draw a bigger circle of love and draw our enemies in. The only way to do that is to forget our dignity and do whatever it takes to get hold of God in our own lives and in the lives of others.

# Chapter 6

# Living the Liberated Life

*Now the Lord is the Spirit; and where the Spirit of the Lord is, there is liberty* (2 Corinthians 3:17).

In a divided society, who is authorized and empowered to model unity? The truth is that only the Church can model the *same unity that exists in Heaven* before the inhabitants of earth. This awesome task is absolutely impossible without God's help.

I believe that history is filled with examples of what happens when the Church timidly pulls back from a controversial problem dividing society and allows an ungodly substitute to fill the gap. This inevitably creates even more division and turmoil. Many church leaders agree that the Church was supposed to take up the battle to restore women to the position of respect, honor, and individual freedom that Jesus demonstrated throughout His unconventional ministry on the earth.

The Church knew the truth about women being co-heirs in Christ. The Church knew the truth that there is neither male nor female, Jew nor Greek, in God's Kingdom; but the Church remained silent and the frustrated and angry voices of feminists stepped in to fill the void in the 1960's. Instead of women being raised up as equal heirs with men, they were positioned as bitter superiors to men who would be better off avoiding long-term heterosexual relationship in marriage.

This new breed of so-called liberated women urged the female half of the human race to "escape" the clutches of motherhood, marriage, femininity, and bras. Millions of young women did just that and inherited all the "benefits" of the false liberty of rebellion: rampant venereal disease through casual sex (which in many cases led to sterility), higher incidences of divorce among those who did marry, and dysfunctional marital relationships in many surviving marriages due to earlier infidelities.

As women began to land jobs and take responsibilities formerly dominated by males, they also began to enjoy higher rates of ulcers, cancer, heart attacks, and strokes that come with the stress of those positions. Sadly, one of the most noticeable fruits of the feminist movement and the bitterness that spawned it is the growing number of wounded women who turn to the lesbian lifestyle hoping to find a replacement for what they rejected as "limiting" and sexist in origin (e.g., monogamous marriage, home, and children).

## God vs. "Jim Crow"

Fortunately, it was Christian men and women who dared to face public anger and hatred in the initial battle for civil rights. The Rev. Dr. Martin Luther King, Jr., was an African-American minister in Atlanta, Georgia, who sincerely loved God. It was his faith in Christ and his deeply held convictions rooted in God's Word that fueled his determined struggle for "equal rights" and personal freedoms for all Americans, regardless of race or color. When he began to organize his non-violent demonstrations against racial prejudice in the United States, the U.S. Constitution and Federal law guaranteed equal rights to everyone. The reality, however, was that millions of African-Americans were still being treated as second-class citizens, forbidden to drink from the same water fountain as "white people."

In many of the southern states, there were numerous municipal and state laws called "Jim Crow laws" that were designed to separate the races. These strictly enforced laws required "colored people" to use separate bathroom facilities and schools, to sit in the back of all public transportation vehicles, or to use "back doors" to public restaurants. A brave young African-American seamstress named Rosa Parks was arrested after she refused a bus driver's command to move to the back of a public transit bus to make room for a boarding white passenger in Montgomery, Alabama, in 1955. This triggered a boycott of the city's bus line, led by Dr. King; it marked the beginning of the modern Civil Rights Movement. Had more violent elements won control of this movement, the entire nation might have been subjected to a terrible bloodbath far worse than anything we actually saw in that era. Praise God that Dr. King's non-violent approach prevailed, and ultimately led to widespread civil rights reform in the U.S.

Throughout those difficult years, the calm voices of Dr. King and other Christian leaders urged civil rights protesters to walk in peace and make their point through strictly non-violent means. They suffered violent attacks by racist crowds and unjust treatment by law enforcement authorities at times, but in the end the quiet voices of godly leaders won the war in the ongoing struggle for racial equality in the United States. In city after city, a small number of white and black churches dared to publicly take a stand for right, and publicly demonstrate God's call for the Church to model reconciliation before the world.

Jesus Christ embodied all the characteristics of a true minister of reconciliation. As we saw in our discussion of Isaiah's prophetic picture of the sevenfold Spirit of God in Isaiah 11, Jesus fulfilled this picture of the Messiah, the first minister of reconciliation, when He came to earth to redeem our race. Paul wrote in Second Corinthians 5:19, "...God was in Christ reconciling the world to Himself, not counting their trespasses against them, and He has committed to us the word of reconciliation." It is our job to cry out to our generation on Christ's behalf, "Be reconciled to God!"

The only true source of "the liberated life" is described by the apostle Paul in a comment made to the church at Corinth: "Now the Lord is the Spirit; and where the Spirit of the Lord is, there is liberty" (2 Cor. 3:17). We can also say it this way: "Where the Lord is the Spirit, or where the Spirit is Lord, then there are people who are genuinely free." You are not free because someone lets you out of jail. You are not free because you have never been in jail. You are free only when you come under the lordship of Jesus Christ and the supreme authority of God the Father.

Jesus Christ was the most liberated person in the universe, and He manifested His liberty on a regular basis by saying such shocking things as, "I only do what the Father tells Me to do. I live My life to please the Father. Whatever pleases the Father pleases Me. My food is to do the will of Him who sent Me and to accomplish His work" (see Jn. 4:34; 5:19,36; 8:28-29). Does it mean that Jesus lived an extraordinarily narrow and ascetic life? No. Does it mean that you have to let God mess up your life and deprive you of everything you really want in order to please Him? No.

The lordship of Jesus frees us when we allow it to rest upon us. I've made up my mind that I want to serve the purpose of God in my life. The next step is to receive the lordship of Jesus without reserve or hesitation. If you really want to understand lordship, then you might want to read some accounts of life in the medieval period in England, France, and Germany. Those countries were largely divided into little independent kingdoms or fiefdoms ruled by lords. These lords owned the land and buildings and ruled the serfs or servants who lived on and in them. They had total power to take any goods they wanted or to exact tariffs or payments from those they ruled. In return, these lords were to provide protection from outside marauders, execute the few laws of the land, and judge between the people when disputes arose. Essentially, the serfs were slaves.

When you come under the lordship of Jesus Christ, you become His slave or servant, His friend, and His adopted sibling all at the same time! Jesus Christ made it clear that *He considered Himself a servant* too. He told His squabbling disciples, "I came not to be served, but to serve" (see Mt. 20:28). Here is one of the most important points in the Bible: We think Jesus meant that He came to serve the masses. He didn't. *Jesus came to serve the purpose of His Father.* Very often, the masses wanted Jesus to stay in one place or another, but He would say something like, "The Father said I must go on to the next city." When He came to the pool of Bethesda where there were many people waiting and hoping to be healed, only one man was healed because that was God's plan for that moment (see Jn. 5:1-9). In other situations, literally everyone who came to Jesus was healed. The different outcomes in each place had to do with God's plan and purpose, not "changing attitudes" on the part of Jesus.

### I Serve for Only One Reason

As a pastor, I serve my congregation in a sense, but I only serve it for one reason: the Father told me to do it. The moment He tells me not to, I'm out of there. If I were to say, "No, Father, I like it so much at that church that I would rather spend my last days there," He might say, "Well, have it your way. Come on home—*right now.*" Jesus Christ was free because He was under the authority of His Father. Jesus had a lot of wisdom, understanding, and counsel. He spoke like no one else in history and performed miracles of all kinds. He had more divine knowledge than anyone else on the earth. It was all there, but it all proceeded from under the Spirit of lordship. We need to remember that everything Jesus accomplished in the earth He did *as a man*, facing the same limitations we do. He demonstrated before us how a man can accomplish superhuman achievements through total submission to the Father in Heaven.

As a model minister of reconciliation, Jesus did three things. First of all, He forgave sins. Second, He repented—even though He didn't need to. Third, He identified with us.

> *I, even I, am the one who wipes out* [blots out—KJV] *your transgressions for My own sake; and **I will not remember your sins**. Put Me in remembrance; let us argue our case together, state your cause, that you may be proved right* (Isaiah 43:25-26).

You might want to underline the passage that declares, "*I will not remember your sins.*" This verse is very important for ministers of reconciliation. The King James Version says God will "blot out" our transgressions. Most people don't know what "blot" means, and the experts are uncertain about whether it means to "black out" or "rub out." One leading authority says, "...erasures in ancient leather scrolls were made by washing or sponging off the ink rather than by blotting. 'Wipe out' is therefore more accurate for the idea of expunge."[1] When God wipes out your sin, no one will ever be able to see it or recognize that it was ever there! If you ask Him why He did this for you, He will tell you what He said through Isaiah thousands of year ago: "I did it for My own sake."

## "Hip-Pocket Forgiveness" Isn't Forgiveness

I especially love what the Lord said next in this passage: "I will not remember your sins" (Is. 43:25b). Most of us have given God a whole lot to remember! We should be very glad that He isn't like us because we just won't let each other forget our sins and failures. We love to practice "hip-pocket forgiveness," where we say, "I forgive you," and put away the memory. But when the person messes up again and asks for forgiveness, we reach back to our "hip pocket" and pull out the police report and say, "But you know the last time...." We store up past transgressions instead of blotting them out, but God says He puts them in what many teachers call "the sea of forgetfulness" (see Mic. 7:19). Corrie ten Boom added, "He puts a sign up for the Pharisees too. It says, *'No fishing.'* "

As ministers of reconciliation, we represent the "Church of the Fresh Start and the Second Chance," but instead we find ourselves shackled to our past in the "Church of the Eternally Damned and the Open Wounds." God says this foolishness *must stop*! A friend of mine from another city accepted the pastorate of a church in suburban Pittsburgh. One of the people he began to minister to was a brother who had been in and out looking for a spiritual pasture to start over in. He just happened to come "back in" when my friend first became the pastor of this church.

During one of the services, my friend tried to commend this man to the congregation, saying, "Now this brother really wants to serve the Lord and we need to encourage him." He didn't know that this man had a long history with the saints before my pastor friend ever got there, but he felt that the Lord wanted to give this brother a fresh new start. While he was describing to the church some of the things that the church needed to do to help reestablish this man, one elderly mother kept rocking back and forth in her pew, waiting for him to get done. He had barely finished when this woman opened her eyes, stopped rocking, and looked at him. In a typical inner-city fashion, she said, "You got to watch Brother Mo, you see...'cause he have did d'is befo." (As if he was the only one....)

Often, when my friends and I remember this classic inner-city quote, we get a great laugh; and yet we are sobered by the fact that many people—urban and suburban—feel this way about broken people. Obviously this woman had overlooked Jesus' instructions about forgiving brothers who have offended us "seventy-times-seven" times (see Mt. 18:22).

**"Because I Said So"**

Since there will never be a shortage of critics and historians who will be quick to rehearse our past sins, failures, and shortcomings to anyone who will listen as well as everyone who doesn't, we can rejoice in one thing: God forgives us and wipes out our sins *for His own sake*. In other words, He never asks our opinion or seeks our permission to forgive and wipe out sins. He doesn't have to because He is God. Isn't it wonderful that God can save people without man's permission? Let me step out on even thinner ice: God can even call people into the ministry without our approval! It doesn't seem to make any difference to God whether or not someone had been divorced five or six times or used to deal drugs five years ago! (I'm not saying that's the norm, but I am saying that God will use anyone and everyone He chooses to use. And if you and I don't like it, we can lump it.)

There are a number of people who don't understand that forgiveness is inextricably bound with healing and restoration. Sometimes it is absolutely impossible to say, "Be healed!" before you say, "You are forgiven." (See the case of the man who was lowered through the roof of a house by his friends in Mark 2:1-12. Jesus declared that his sins were forgiven before He pronounced him healed.) The Church needs to get in touch with what the ministry of reconciliation is. When Jesus the God/Man was saying to the man on the stretcher, "Your sins are forgiven," it wasn't just Jesus speaking to the man, it was *God* in Christ (the same God who dwells in you and I).

## Ugly to the Bone

The people who object to the ministry of reconciliation the most are modern-day Sadducees and Pharisees. They seem to be "the same yesterday, today, and forever" with almost the same consistency as God. We have Pharisees in our churches and visiting our churches today, and they still pray the same way they did in Jesus' day: "God, I thank You that I am not like others." I can almost hear God replying, "I've got news for you. If you have eyeballs, hair, and teeth—whether you bought them or grew them—if you have human blood in your veins, then you are like 'the others.' You may not think you are, but you are. Have you heard the expression, 'beauty is only skin deep, but ugly is all the way to the bone'? You were born into sin, and sin is ugly all the way to the bone."

There are certain things that you can't get rid of, no matter how much you powder it, shape it, skin it, liposuction it, operate on it, or bleach it. It doesn't change. Thank God that the Scriptures tell us:

*And He will delight in the fear of the Lord, and He will not judge by what His eyes see, nor make a decision by what His ears hear; but with righteousness He will judge the poor, and decide with fairness for the afflicted of the earth....* (Isaiah 11:3-4).

I think God loves you just like you are. He probably "wonders" why you do some of the things you do sometimes, but God is not "uptight" in Heaven. He is not holding a strike against people who get weird haircuts with odd colors or shaved lines in their heads anymore than He does those who are angry about painful incidents in their past. However, He is concerned about the sins we are clinging to.

## It's a Tough Day for Wrinkles

God wants to present to Himself a glorious Church without spot or wrinkle, but I don't think He intends to wait until the last minute to somehow zap us with a "spiritual micro-wave" for a quick fix. He is cleaning up *now* and He isn't us-ing a washing machine. He is using one of those scrub boards where you have to rub extra hard on stains, wrin-kles, and other problem areas. "What are you doing that for, God?" He says, "Because I am washing you with the water of the Word so that I can present to Myself a glorious Church without spot or wrinkle or blemish or any such thing" (see Eph. 5:25-27). "What's my job?" we ask. "Your job is *to do what Jesus did*," the Father says. What did He do? He forgave sins.

More of us are "Simon Peters" today than we care to ad-mit. You remember Peter, don't you? When Jesus warned the disciples that they all would forsake and betray Him in His final hours, Peter the rock, the brave one, said (accord-ing to the "Garlington Summarized Freestyle Version"), "No way. Not me. If You are going to die, then I'm going with You. If it is going to cost You Your life, then it is going to cost mine" (see Lk. 22:31-34). Jesus said, "Peter, time out. Even before the rooster crows in the morning, you are going to deny Me three times." Jesus looked at him and said, "I want to clue you in on this: satan actually asked Me for you, so I have prayed particularly for you, Peter, that your faith will not fail you." Here is the key. Jesus said, "But I have prayed for you, that your faith may not fail; and you, *when once you have turned again* [repented], strengthen your broth-ers" (Lk. 22:32).

Did Peter deny Jesus? Yes, and he even did it with an oath to God like we hear so often in the world, "I swear to God I don't know that guy! I don't know who you are talking about!" (see Mt. 26:74) Your speech will betray you. Once you get in the church you can't forget the lingo. It slips out every now and then. If someone comes up on you while you are doing some drugs in the bathroom and says, "How is it going?" you might just say, "Praise the Lord." (God doesn't leave you just because you leave Him. He camps on your doorstep and hounds and bothers you until you change your mind about the dumb decisions you have made.)

**Forgiven and Called to Forgive**

Jesus looked Peter in the eye when he denied Him for the third and last time (see Lk. 22:61-62). Guilt almost destroyed the man in the hours that led up to the Lord's death and ultimate resurrection. Who was the object of the Lord's most piercing and intimate conversation after His resurrection? *Peter.* The true nature of the Lord's ministry of reconciliation is seen clearly in John 21:15-19. Jesus didn't pin Peter to the ground and shout, "You betrayed Me! You aren't fit to bear My name anymore. You aren't fit for the ministry. You aren't even fit to be in My Kingdom!" No, Jesus gently and persistently steered Peter's eyes back to the task of tending the Lord's sheep—as a minister of reconciliation. The forgiven are called to forgive. The "failed" are called to gather and tend other failures in God's tender love and forgiveness.

I am an ambassador and minister of forgiveness. My chief credential is the fact that I have been forgiven by my loving Lord, and He has sent me to tell you that He forgives you too. You are a minister of reconciliation and forgiveness too, and you have the same credentials. Jesus said, "If you forgive the sins of any, their sins have been forgiven them; if you retain the sins of any, they have been retained" (Jn. 20:23). How many times have you read these words of Jesus? Did you assume these words were only addressed to the 12 disciples? Don't. They apply to everyone who has been given the ministry of reconciliation. People need to hear the good news that God forgives them, and they need to hear it from you, from *someone who has been forgiven*.

Most people outside of God's Kingdom think of God in terms of the Ten Commandments. They think that the

"God-kind-of-life" is a life locked in to the "Ten 'Thou Shalt Nots.' " You can't blame them, because that's mostly what we tell them! The problem is that Jesus wasn't content to say it that way. A theologian, a "doctor of the Jewish law," asked Jesus, "Which is the greatest commandment?"

> *Jesus answered, "The foremost is, 'HEAR, O ISRAEL! THE LORD OUR GOD IS ONE LORD; AND YOU SHALL LOVE THE LORD YOUR GOD WITH ALL YOUR HEART, AND WITH ALL YOUR SOUL, AND WITH ALL YOUR MIND, AND WITH ALL YOUR STRENGTH.' The second is this, 'YOU SHALL LOVE YOUR NEIGHBOR AS YOURSELF.' There is no other commandment greater than these"* (Mark 12:29-31).

People all around you are desperate to know why you are happy. They know you aren't perfect, but they are puzzled at how you keep going when you face the same problems they face. You have the opportunity to extend God's forgiveness while you are sitting at your computer terminal, typewriter, or steering wheel, or while you work at your production line or exercise at the gym. Jesus didn't forgive you just to "take you out of the world." He did just the opposite. He prayed that His Father *would not* take you out of the world! (see Jn. 17:15) Jesus gave you the power to live the liberated life *in front of people living enslaved lives*. Why? So you can set them free in His name and power!

We are not accustomed to good news. We don't believe in getting it, and we don't believe in giving it. But this is God's good news for us all: "I blotted out your transgressions for My own sake and I will not remember your sins any longer." He is sending you out to the world to live an openly liberated life with a powerful message, and the Moslems need to hear it: "God has forgiven you." People of every color and culture need to hear it: "God has forgiven you." Feminists and male chauvinists need to hear it: "God has forgiven you! Taste the truly liberated life in Jesus." It all begins the same way—when we become reconciled to God.

### Endnote

1. Walter C. Kaiser, Ph.D., Dean and Chairman of the Old Testament and Semitic Languages, Trinity Evangelical Divinty School, as quoted by R. Laird Harris, Gleason L. Archer, Jr., and Bruce K. Waltke, eds., *Theological Wordbook of the Old Testament*, Vol. I (Chicago: Moody Press, 1980), 498, definition #1178 for *maha*, "I, wipe, wipe out."

# Chapter 7

# See the Tower
# That God Is Building

When Adam fell through sin, he messed up more than his own life; he messed up the whole earth. That is why we read in Romans chapter 8 that *all creation* is waiting for the manifestation or revealing of the sons of God. It's not just men and women, boys and girls, but all creation—including the lions, the gorillas, the baboons, the chimpanzees, the leopards, the cheetahs, the elephants, and the physical earth itself.

> *For the anxious longing of the creation waits eagerly for the revealing of the sons of God. For the creation was subjected to futility, not of its own will, but because of Him who subjected it, in hope that the creation itself also will be set free from its slavery to corruption into the freedom of the glory of the children of God. For we know that the whole creation groans and suffers the pains of childbirth together until now* (Romans 8:19-22).

All of creation is groaning and asking us, "Look, why don't you people get your act together?" Paul gave us a picture of someone waiting on tiptoes when he said all creation is "anxiously longing" and "waiting eagerly." The entire world is saying, "When are you people ever going to come and help get us sorted out?" (This isn't a request for a "rapture drill"; it's a request to hear the gospel of hope and to see it lived out in real life.)

God is reconciling us and the world to Himself. Look at this quote entitled "The Actual and the Ideal."

> "There are two things, the *actual* and the *ideal*. To be mature is to see the ideal and live with the actual. To fail is to accept the actual and reject the ideal. And to accept only that which is ideal and refuse the actual is to be immature. Do not criticize the actual because you have seen the ideal. Do not reject the ideal because you see the actual. Maturity is to *live with the actual* but *hold on to the ideal* (emphasis added)."[1]

What do we do with the ministry of reconciliation? In a divided society the Church must model unity. To put it in a more personal way, "In a divided society, *I* must do *my part* to model unity." The big challenge we face as ministers of reconciliation is that we are constantly confronted by the *actual* situation on earth while trying to model the *ideal* that we find in Scripture. We are constantly praying, "God, how can we reconcile these two?" That is what the ministry of reconciliation is all about.

We are called to obey God above all, but how can we obey Him if we don't understand what it is that we are supposed to do? Let me illustrate this from the Garlington family storybook. Say that for some reason you come up to me with the news that you have found a piece of clay that has just been "smushed," as our kids used to say. Then for an equally strange reason I say, "Would you make this all over again for me? Thanks." Naturally you would reply, "Do what?" When I repeat my request that you reform the piece of clay, you look closely at it again, but all you see is "smush." Assuming that you are the type of person who is kind to the chronically confused, you will ask me a very logical question at that point, "Garlington, I'll do my best to reform this piece of clay. *But what did it look like before it was smushed?*"

How would you feel if I said, "Well, that's easy. It kind of looked like a little bit of this [as I gesture vaguely in the air], and had some of this on it [as I pluck at an invisible something or other], and it was about 'so big' right in here" [as I take the classic 'proud fisherman's pose' to demonstrate something that appears much larger than in real life]. I can guarantee you that you would be feeling very frustrated at this point as you held that ridiculous piece of smushed clay. That's the way people in the world feel about Jesus and the Church. They want details and pictures, but all we give them are generalized descriptions of God and His Kingdom.

People don't want fuzzy and contradictory descriptions of God. They want us to give them a model, a clear picture of God at work in the earth. Frankly, most if not all people secretly hope that God really is real, but they are afraid of being disappointed. *Now we can be a model* because God's Word says we can. In fact, we are to be examples of Christ's walk in the earth. The reason the followers of Jesus were first called "Christians" in Antioch was because the very word means "like Christ" (see Acts 11:26). Now those are some big shoes to fill.

Now the onus or burden of all this isn't on us as much as it is on Christ. After all, He lets us call ourselves Christians, even when we don't really live up to that high standard all the time. He isn't like us, because the Bible says, "For the gifts and the calling of God are irrevocable" (Rom. 11:29). Now when our kids do well in public competition or performance, we heap on the praise and tell all our friends, "That's my girl there. Did you see her break that long jump record?" "That's my boy. He averages 30 points per game—on his bad days." But what do we do when they mess up? "Hey, is that your son?" "Where? Who are you talking about?" We don't want to identify with people and their failures, but

Jesus willingly calls us "Christian" from the very beginning—even though He knows that we probably won't be the very best models of Christianity (especially in our early days of the faith).

He wants us to understand what He means by reconciliation, and that He intends to reconcile *all things* to Himself. He wants us to understand what God is *taking us back to*. As we noted in earlier chapters, Paul told the Corinthians, "Now all these things are from God, who reconciled us to Himself through Christ, and gave us the ministry of reconciliation" (2 Cor. 5:18). The Greek word translated as "reconcile," *katallasso*, means "to effect a change, to exchange."[2] The term appears with a preposition and tense form that strengthens the phrase to read, "Now all these things are from God, who effected in us a *thorough change back* to Himself through Christ." W.E. Vine says the same word was used in First Corinthians 7:11 to refer to a woman returning to her husband.[3] Reconciliation with God obviously isn't something that takes place between equals. God doesn't have to be reconciled to us—we are the ones who wandered and fell. We have to be reconciled back to Him, and He was the only one powerful enough to do it.

## The Chevy and the Cadillac

Iraneus, one of the early church fathers, had a theory that he called the "recapitulation theory." Doesn't that bless you? It will once you figure out what in the world he was talking about. Iraneus taught that Jesus Christ came to give back to us everything that Adam lost through his sin in the Garden of Eden. So when Jesus is reconciling us, He is not simply getting us to "shake hands with God" and saying it's all better. He makes us new creatures, not merely remade or repaired beings. He always leaves us better than before we met Him.

Imagine for a moment that you have wrecked your beloved Chevrolet. Your insurance estimator looks at it and says, "This car is totaled. There is nothing that can be done for it." You have just accurately pictured the way you and I appeared when God looked at us before we surrendered to Jesus. "This life is totaled. There is nothing that can be done for it in the natural. It is beyond repair." You would probably say, "Well, what do I do?"

Now imagine your insurance representative tells you, "How about taking the keys to this brand-new car?" When we ask what can be done, God says something that no insurance adjuster in his right mind would ever say to an earthly customer: "Here is your key to a new life in Christ." "But God, I totaled a Chevrolet. This is the key to a new Cadillac!" He says, "That's all right." You'd accept that kind of deal, wouldn't you? That's a picture of what God means when He says, "If any man be in Christ, he is a new creature" (2 Cor. 5:17 KJV). You are not just something that He worked over and patched up. He didn't restore you, remake you, reconstruct you, or remodel you. He *reconciled* you by making you a totally new creature. And this is what we mean when we tell others, "Be reconciled to God."

Reconciliation goes a step beyond Iraneus' recapitulation theory, because Jesus does far more than restore the relationship Adam had with God. Jesus Christ restores us back to God's original intent for us, the destiny that Adam never got to fulfill because sin interrupted his progress. Most of us think and act like God is simply remaking us in a Holy Ghost reform school of some sort. But God isn't interested in just saying, "Let Me tweak this, adjust that, and change that." No, He chucks the old and creates something brand-new! When He reconciles us to Himself, He is reconciling us to the image *of how He sees us*. Here we bump into our old challenge again: God sees us as we shall be—the *ideal*. We see ourselves as we were or as we are—the *actual*. God isn't loving what you see;

He gave His life for it, but He knows what needs to be done to make you fit for eternal life in His presence. It requires nothing less than reconciliation by re-creation to conform us to the image of Jesus:

> *For it was the Father's good pleasure for all the fulness to dwell in Him, and through Him to reconcile all things to Himself, having made peace through the blood of His cross; through Him, I say, whether things on earth or things in heaven* (Colossians 1:19-20).

> *For whom He foreknew, He also predestined **to become conformed to the image of His Son**, that He might be the first-born among many brethren* (Romans 8:29).

Paul tells us more about what God is reconciling us to and why in the Book of Ephesians:

> *For **we are His workmanship**, created in Christ Jesus for good works, which God prepared beforehand, that we should walk in them. ... remember that you [Gentiles] were at that time separate from Christ, excluded from the commonwealth of Israel, and strangers to the covenants of promise, having no hope and without God in the world. But now in Christ Jesus you who formerly were far off have been brought near by the blood of Christ. For He Himself is our peace, who made both groups into one, and broke down the barrier of the dividing wall, **by abolishing in His flesh the enmity**, which is the Law of commandments contained in ordinances, that in Himself He might make the two **into one new man**, thus establishing peace, and might reconcile them both in one body to God through the cross, **by it having put to death the enmity**. ... So then you are no longer strangers and aliens, but you are fellow citizens with the saints, and are of God's household* (Ephesians 2:10,12-16,19).

We are God's workmanship, His wonderful masterpiece, created in Christ Jesus for good works. You and I are not created for anything other than good works, so if we are doing anything other than good works, we are at cross purposes with our reason for existence. Most of the world is at "cross purposes" with God's purposes. Look at the little word *enmity*. Very few people really understand what it means, but we're going to be in that number.

Whether you look at the English word *enmity* or its original Greek equivalent *echtra*, both terms come from their respective root words for "enemy." *Enmity* is "positive, active, and typically mutual hatred or ill will."[4] At one time, all of us were without Christ. We were illegal aliens ineligible for fellowship with our Creator, having no hope. We were shut off from the things that God was doing for His people because our sin created *enmity* between us and the unchanging God. But then we were supernaturally brought near to God by the blood of Christ. Jesus reconciled us to God in one body through the cross—thereby *putting to death the enmity*.

One problem area we face is that when we come to know the Lord and allow Him to transform our lives, we think all our hang-ups and problems will be gone when we finally get home that day. However, they are still there in most cases, except one component has changed. There is a new creature inside, but the new creature still lives in the same body he or she had before getting saved. If your body happened to like cigarettes or had a habit of stealing things before you got saved, then don't be surprised if you find the hands attached to that body reaching for a cigarette or snatching something from a store shelf the day after you are saved. We have to work on certain things to bring the *actual* up to par with God's *ideal*. If, before you were saved, you had a habit of kicking your dog every time he barked, then you will probably have to deal with your automatic response to the dog's barking—even though the Holy Spirit of God now dwells in your heart. All of us have some habits and appetites that weren't completely obliterated when we received salvation through Christ.

Enmity exists between males and females, between ethnic and racial groups, between social and economic classes, between blondes and brunettes, between people who wear glasses and those who don't, and between people with hair and those without hair. We have all kinds of outward distinctions in society that effectively divide us. Jesus wants to destroy that enmity, but we have to cooperate with Him.

## Climbing to the Top of the Heap

The antagonism society produces is *not* the result of something that God has done. Antagonism and enmity are the result of something that sin has done. Sin makes us unconsciously grasp and struggle to regain what was irretrievably lost in the Garden of Eden, our "first estate" as sons of God. It is impossible for us to get this back without God's help, but if we don't know or acknowledge this fact, then we just keep on fighting to reach "the top of the heap" at any cost. It got so bad early in human history that God had to step in.

> *Now these are the records of the generations of Shem, Ham, and Japheth, the sons of Noah; and sons were born to them after the flood. ... These are the families of the sons of Noah, according to their genealogies, by their nations; and out of these the nations were separated on the earth after the flood. Now the whole earth used the same language and the same words. And it came about as they journeyed east, that they found a plain in the land of Shinar and settled there. And they said to one another, "Come, let us make bricks and burn them thoroughly." And they used brick for stone, and they used tar for mortar. And they said, "Come, let us build for ourselves a city, and a tower whose top will reach into heaven, and let us make for ourselves a name; lest we be scattered abroad over the face of the whole earth." And the Lord came down to see the city and the tower which the sons of men had built. And the Lord said, "Behold, they are one*

*people, and they all have the same language. And this is what they began to do, and now nothing which they purpose to do will be impossible for them. Come, let Us go down and there confuse their language, that they may not understand one another's speech." So the Lord scattered them abroad from there over the face of the whole earth; and they stopped building the city. Therefore its name was called Babel, because there the Lord confused the language of the whole earth; and from there the Lord scattered them abroad over the face of the whole earth* (Genesis 10:1,32–11:1-9).

When the Lord came down to see the city and the tower that "the sons of men" had built, He was checking up on the offspring of Shem, Ham, and Japheth, the sons of Noah. Notice that it was *God*, not Moses, who said, "Behold, they are one people, and they all have the same language. And this is what they began to do, and now nothing which they purpose to do will be impossible for them" (Gen. 11:6). That is when God said, "Come, let Us go down and there confuse their language, that they may not understand one another's speech" (Gen. 11:7).

Just think about why God confused the common speech of mankind. He did it because when they were in unity, nothing that they purposed to do would be *impossible* for them. It was God who planted that potential in us in the first place, but He always intended for that potential to be tapped *in harmony with His purposes and in unity with His heart*. The issue isn't that God doesn't want us to accomplish great things. He just doesn't want us to organize ourselves apart from His lordship.

When God visited His creations on the plain of Shinar, He said, "These guys are getting ready to do something that I don't want them to do. Humanity is trying to organize itself apart from Me to win a name for itself." (Doesn't that sound familiar? That is exactly what lucifer tried to do just before he was booted out of Heaven faster than the speed of light.)

In my opinion, that is also what the United Nations is trying to do: organize humanity *apart from God*. Frankly, any effort that seeks to bring people together apart from the lordship of Jesus Christ is a problem to God, and He will move Heaven and earth to disperse it and keep it in confusion.

> *The God who made the world and all things in it, since He is Lord of heaven and earth, does not dwell in temples made with hands; neither is He served by human hands, as though He needed anything, since He Himself gives to all life and breath and all things; and He made from one, every nation of mankind to live on all the face of the earth, having determined their appointed times, and the boundaries of their habitation, that they should seek God, if perhaps they might grope for Him and find Him, though He is not far from each one of us; for in Him we live and move and exist, as even some of your own poets have said, "For we also are His offspring"* (Acts 17:24-28).

Now what is God's hope? He is seeking those who will worship Him in spirit and in truth (see Jn. 4:23). There is a longing inside every human being to discover and reunite with the Creator. That explains why successful business leaders, Ph.D.'s, and wealthy aristocrats all end up at seminars where they hand over $500 a head to hear some fast-talking guru of good-feel say, "I know how to give you peace and success. Memorize this little secret word, then open your mouth really wide so your 'spirit guide' can come in [which is really your own personal demon spirit]. Your guide will show you how to conduct your business and achieve success."

Why would anyone seriously consider paying cash to be possessed by a familiar spirit? (People in the world call this "channeling.") The answer is simple. These intelligent and sincere people are simply trying to find God. They are "groping" to find their Maker, and they are having a difficult time because they are so broken and have fallen so far from their "first estate." Praise God that He doesn't leave us groping in the dark: "For the Son of Man has come to seek and to save that which was lost" (Lk. 19:10).

Jesus entered human society and said, "Here I am," and they said, "No, You can't be the Messiah. You don't look like what we think God should look like. And You definitely don't act like God would act if He was really here! Besides, God would never speak to Samaritans. We don't, so surely God doesn't." From the beginning, men have busied themselves drawing smaller and smaller circles to exclude people they don't like, but God had a plan to wipe out those circles of hatred drawn in the dust. He drew a great big circle in the sand of our planet using His own blood. Then He invited *everyone* inside.

## Babel Divides, the Spirit Unites

On the Day of Pentecost in Acts 2, God reversed the curse of Babel and revealed the original purpose for man's ability to communicate, unite, and change the world. Why? Because *under the lordship of Jesus Christ*, it is *good* for us to speak the same thing in perfect unity with no division among us. Although *Babel divides, Pentecost unites.* God had drawn people out of every tongue, every tribe, every kindred, and every place where people lived and placed them together in Jerusalem so they could hear an unlearned fisherman declare the good news of Jesus Christ. His message was echoed by 120 people speaking of the marvelous works of God in every tongue represented there that day (see Acts 2:5-12). God was unifying mankind again through the unified declaration of the gospel of Jesus Christ.

This was made more amazing because most of the 120 people were evidently Galileans, which linguistically must have been the equivalent of a "mid-Tennessee" or "central Mississippi" accent. It was impossible for these people to speak foreign languages (if they knew them in the first place) without carrying a heavy Galilean accent into their speech.

Typical Galileans couldn't hide their accent even if they wanted to, but evidently these people were speaking totally foreign languages perfectly (and miraculously). *God, what are You doing?* "I am bringing people together." *God, what are You about?* "I am reconciling and restoring My creation back to a complete state of harmony."

First God had to divide our languages and races because we were not walking under His lordship, and we were determined to become our own god by building occult towers to ascend to the heavens by our own efforts. (It didn't work then, and it still doesn't work today.) The human race is still trying to reach Heaven through "do-it-yourself, worship yourself" religious manipulation (we call it by the overly polite name, "New Age Movement"). No matter what you call it, the New Age Movement is occult in origin. It is a rainbow coalition of mankind massing themselves under the banner of rebellion apart from the lordship of Jesus Christ. As believers, we have no choice. We can't be a part of it because we belong to a new society that has a supernatural distinctive. It has eternal values, divine purpose, and divine order in the harmony of sacrificial love. It has a king and a lord, and it has a commonwealth and citizenry. We even have a country, but we have no right to "vote."

There are no votes in the Kingdom of God. The theme song of the Kingdom is, "Yes, Lord, yes Lord, from the bottom of my heart to the depths of my soul, yes, Lord."[5] Why? Because God has said:

> *And He said to him, " 'YOU SHALL LOVE THE LORD YOUR GOD WITH ALL YOUR HEART, AND WITH ALL YOUR SOUL, AND WITH ALL YOUR MIND.' This is the great and foremost commandment. The second is like it, 'YOU SHALL LOVE YOUR NEIGHBOR AS YOURSELF.' On these two commandments depend the whole Law and the Prophets"* (Matthew 22:37-40).

What does God want in His Church? Paul put it this way: "Now I exhort you, brethren, by the name of our Lord Jesus Christ, that you all agree, and there be *no divisions* [male/female, race, social/economic, tongue] among you, but you be made complete in the same mind and in the same judgment" (1 Cor. 1:10). Why? Because if we all start speaking the same thing, nothing will be impossible to us. Now do you see why satan doesn't want us to speak the same thing? Where just two or three gather together in Jesus' name, He will manifest Himself right there among them. It's even better than that. Jesus said that when we actually touch and agree about anything that we ask Him, it will be done (see Mt. 18:19-20). *All we have to do is agree.*

As mentioned before, one pastor's "translation" of verse 20 says, "If two or three of you *ever* get together, *I'll come to see it Myself*"! The enemy is determined to keep us apart, and he will create all kinds of confusion just to keep us separated. Many times he focuses his efforts on our fears of rejection, whispering slander in our ears, "They don't like me. In fact, they never did like me. That's okay, because I don't like them either."

A mother woke up her son one morning and said, "It's time to go to church, son." He said from under his covers, "I don't want to go!" The mother answered, "But you have to go. Get up." He said, "No, I don't want to go." Finally the mother said, "Give me two reasons why you shouldn't go." He said, "I don't like them, and they don't like me. Now you give me two reasons why I *should* go." She said, "Because you are 40 years old, and because you are the pastor of the church."

Too many of us move through life with a paranoia that "people don't like us." Let's stop thinking about people and just get together in the family of God. The apostle John warned Christ's followers, "Do not marvel, brethren, if the world hates you" (1 Jn. 3:13). It's not just an issue of Republican and

Democrat, liberal and conservative, wealthy or poor, or black, white, Hispanic, or Asian. The hatred of the world springs directly from the realm of spiritual warfare. "Why are they hating me? I thought that after Jesus came into my life, that if I just loved everybody, then they would love me back." That's the ideal. Following is a picture of the actual: On your first day back at your job after you came from the altar the night before, where you were washed in the cleansing fountain of Jesus' blood, where your soul was filled and your face took on a happy glow—*somebody is going to spot that glow on your face.* Without your even saying a word, somebody will notice that you are different. He or she will ask, "What's wrong with you?" When you say, "I just became a Christian," that co-worker will launch the familiar tirade: "Oh, *one of those.* Born again, huh? Very funny. Where's your Bible?"

The hatred of the world is understandable, but hatred within the Church is unspeakable. You and I should be able to get along and our outward distinctions shouldn't keep us apart. Our major task is to model something of our new life in Christ before we tell people what they ought to be. God is saying that the issue is not, "Will the Church and the world ever be reconciled?" The issue for us is even more basic than that right now. It is, "Can the Church be reconciled to itself? Can we start loving one another as God wants us to love one another?" We can change some of our differences, and others we can't. The bottom line is that our common life in Christ is greater than any difference that exists between us! God is giving us no room for excuses. He expects us to model Christ's life for the world. They need to see us fellowship, pray, and play together in genuine love. The lost need to see us having a wonderful time and enjoying life with other Christians. We can't turn it around by ourselves, but we can make a difference if together we'll display the grace and glory of God as one body.

After the stage in our newly built sanctuary was carpeted, a Yamaha grand piano was sitting on the floor that had to be moved up to the stage. One strong man by himself couldn't have moved it into place, so we all got together and concluded that we had enough willing hands and backs to do it. One thing remained: We all had to speak the same language about the task. That huge piano would still be on the floor if we had all stood around asking one another, "What are you going to do? Oh no, I'm not taking that end…" No, we came into agreement and spoke the same thing. "You guys get on the back side, some of you take the front side, and on the count of three, we lift together and bring it onto the stage." We moved together exactly as we said we would. As a result, what would have been a massive effort for a few staff members became a very easy and quick task accomplished with a larger body in unity.

Each of us will have the opportunity to speak or do deeds as a little light or candle of the Lord's presence. But God wants to bring us together. He says, "I want you to be more than a candle. I want you to be a city set on a hill that cannot be hid" (see Mt. 5:14). In the Book of Genesis, humanity said, "Come now, let us build a tower," and they built a monstrosity to elevate themselves to the heavens (see Gen. 11:4). In our generation, we must say, "Come now, let us work together to lift Jesus higher until the whole earth is covered with His glory."

### Endnotes

1. Excerpted from a sermon by Charles Simpson. Used by permission.

2. W.E. Vine, Merrill F. Unger, William White, Jr., *Vine's Complete Expository Dictionary of Old and New Testament Words* (Nashville, Tennessee: Thomas Nelson Publishers, 1985), 513-514, adapted from entries for "reconcile" (Greek: *katallasso*), "reconciliation" (Greek: *apokatallasso*).

3. Vine, *Vine's Complete Expository Dictionary*, 514, stated at the end of note 1 under *katallasso* (reconcile).

4. *Merriam-Webster's Collegiate Dictionary*, 10th ed. (Springfield, Massachusetts: Merriam-Webster, Inc., 1994), 385, *enmity*.

5. Excerpted from Sandra Crouch, "Completely Yes" ©1985 Bud John Songs, Sanabella Music.

# Chapter 8

# Have You Seen God's Tribulator?

Have you ever sensed the overwhelming feeling come over you that God loves you? If you have, then you know it is impossible to explain it. God has a way of communicating directly to the deepest part of you, and there is no way to describe how it feels. One time I was right in the middle of a tremendous worship time in a service when I sensed the Lord say, "Tell them how much I love them. But don't just tell them—*sing it.*" So I stood up and I began to sing, "If you only knew how much I love you…"

I honestly don't believe that we have digested the reality that God isn't merely putting up with us—*He loves us*. He isn't looking at the world and saying, "I can't wait until I send My Son back so I can wipe out all the rest of those buzzards who rejected Me!" That's something *we* would do, but it is not what God is doing. His heart aches for the world. He sent us to the world with a bold message for the unsaved: "God says He is not counting your trespasses against you!"

What a powerful privilege it is to share good news with people who are flailing in messes of their own making, who feel caught and trapped with no way of escape, like they are gripped by some kind of vortex that is taking them down,

down, down. Feeling helpless, they spin, kick, scream, and knock down anybody who comes near them. You and I have the one message that will change all that. We need to come to them and say, "Hey, I need to tell you something: God's not counting your sins against you." We can witness a miracle as they shake off their terror and ask, "You mean God cares about me—even in the middle of all this mess that I've made?" Yes!

I want to say two important things to you right now:

*First of all*, if God cared enough to die for you even when you hated Him, how much more does He care for you now that He's adopted you into His family? Jesus was sent to display God's love to you so that you could be saved and become part of His family.

*Second*, He is sending *you* into the world to do the same by modeling reconciliation, and it is a serious assignment. John the Baptist said, "...He who is coming after me is mightier than I, and I am not fit to remove His sandals; He will baptize you with the Holy Spirit *and fire*. And His winnowing fork is in His hand, and He will thoroughly clear His threshing floor; and He will gather His wheat into the barn, but He will burn up the chaff with unquenchable fire" (Mt. 3:11-12).

A winnowing fork was something farmers used in Jesus' day to separate wheat grains from chaff. Chaff is the outer sheath that surrounds the head or grains of wheat in the growth process. The chaff actually protects the wheat grain as it grows and becomes mature. When the wheat reaches maturity, whole stalks were brought to a hard, uneven piece of ground called a threshing floor. Then the workers brought in sticks or a shovel-like implement called a "tribulator." (The English word *tribulation* literally came from the Latin root *tribulare*, which meant "to press, oppress"; and from *tribulum*, which was a drag used in threshing.[1]) This

"tribulator" is what the Bible calls a winnowing fan or winnowing fork, and it was used to beat the chaff off the wheat.
Once they were separated, the wheat was gathered into the
barn and the chaff was taken somewhere else to be burned.

### What Are the Crispy Critters?

We used to think of the wheat grain as "the good guys"
and considered the chaff to be "the bad guys" who became
crispy critters. But in reality, the wheat grains and the chaff
together were the "good guys," and the tares (weeds) were
"the bad guys." The wheat is first separated from the tares,
and then the tares are burned. The wheat and the chaff are
also separated, but they are separated in a different way. You
can't burn the chaff and spare the wheat unless you first *beat
the chaff off* of the wheat. You probably won't want to hear
how this applies to you, but I'll tell you anyway.

When you are growing up in God, He puts up with a lot
of garbage in your life in the early days because He knows
that He's going to get you to the threshing floor eventually—
along with all the stuff that is going on in your life. Now, He
has a particular way of getting the garbage out of your life,
even though it often surrounds the kernel of life He's
planted within you. He uses a little device we'll call "the
tribulator." The process is simple and effective. You put the
wheat and chaff down and you beat it. Another way of saying
it is this: *You get your chicken kicked* (see Chapter 2).

God is showing us that there are certain things that He
no longer finds acceptable in our lives. We read in Matthew's Gospel (3:11) that Jesus has come to baptize us with
the Holy Spirit (and we say, "Thank You, Jesus!" before we
notice the last word) *and fire*. Well, what is this "fire" business? We think this "fire" thing has come to make us enthu-
siastic. Maybe the fire comes to make us more powerful
witnesses, or to give us great big chill bumps instead of the

little ones. Some people think the fire comes so that we can sense more powerfully the presence of God.

News Flash: *The fire comes to get the junk out of your life.* If you think you are going to walk with God and not ever have the fire anoint your backside, then you probably need to sit down and pray Elijah's prayer and get it over with. Elijah was fed up with God's tribulator and tribulation in general. As soon as he'd finished the meal God had sent him using angelic caterers, Elijah went to a cave and began to complain about how hard his life was (see 1 Kings 19). He was basically saying, "Lord, it's enough. *Take me home.*" That's what you have to pray if you don't like the way God is making you a better representative to the world. You need to be honest and tell God, "I think I've had as much of this blessing as I can stand. Just let me have one little isolated mini-rapture and get me right on out of here." The problem is that God has a bigger agenda than we do. God answered Elijah by telling him who would be his *replacement* (see 1 Kings 19:16).

If you're not ready to check out of here right now, then don't be surprised if God sees something in your life that He has tolerated for a few years but is saying now, "It is time for that chaff to go." You will know it is time for it to go when you begin to feel the "fires of cleansing" warming up the edges of your life. If you really want to be an authentic minister of reconciliation, then every now and then God will have to point out certain things in your life that have to go.

**Driving in Style**

A friend who was a Roman Catholic priest once told me the joke of the time the pope was scheduled to deliver a very important speech to the delegates of the United Nations in New York City. Unfortunately, it was impossible for the pontiff's plane to land at JFK International Airport due to air traffic congestion. In desperation, the officials said, "Land in

Newark and we will provide a limousine there to whisk you back through the city and get you to the U.N. building so you can give your speech."

When the pope came out of the airport at Newark, the limousine was there waiting for him and he said to the driver, "My son, I really need you not to spare anything, but get me to my appointment. This is a very important speech I am about to make." The driver of the limousine said, "Holy Father, I need to tell you that I already have several marks against my license, and I cannot afford to get one more mark. I can't speed. I just can't afford to do that." Hearing this, the pope said, "Would you mind if I drove?" Then the surprised driver said, "Sure, you can drive."

So the chauffeur got in the back of the long limousine and the pope moved into the driver's seat. He hadn't driven himself for some time, but before long he was driving as though he had the freedom to drive as fast and as freely as he felt was necessary. When he reached the Big Apple, two of New York's finest cops were patrolling the area in their squad car when they spotted the limousine doing things they had never seen any limousine do in New York City before (and *that's* saying something). So they quickly pursued the limousine and signaled the driver to pull over. The officer driving the car stepped out with his ticket book while the other remained behind to check in with precinct headquarters by radio.

The officer with the ticket book walked toward the limousine and was just about to write the ticket, but when he walked up to the driver's door, the window rolled down and he just stood there in shocked disbelief for a moment. His partner in the squad car watched in amazement as the officer shook his head, put his ticket book back in his pocket, and came back to the squad car.

"Why didn't you give the guy a ticket?" his partner asked. The officer shook his head again and said, "Somebody *really important* is in that car." The partner said, "How important could he be? Is he more important than the mayor of New York?" The officer said, "Oh, he is definitely more important than the mayor of New York." Baffled, the man's partner said, "Is he more important than the *governor* of New York?" The officer nodded and said, "I'm telling you this guy is more important than the governor of New York!" Now it was really getting confusing. There was only one place to go. "Are you telling me he is more important than the *President of the United States?*" Incredibly, the officer nodded again and said, "This guy is even more important than the President of the United States!"

"Who on earth could be more important than the President of the United States?" the partner asked. The police officer shook his head and said, "I honestly don't know. But I'll tell you what—*the pope is his chauffeur!*"

**Now God Has Sent *You***

You are probably asking a question of your own at this point: "Garlington, what in the world is your point in all this?" *My point in all this is that Jesus is your chauffeur.* He is personally taking you through life, and just the sheer fact that the King of glory wants to lead us and care for us is a weighty proposition in itself. He is expressing an undying concern for His people and for His flock, but He is also saying to us, "I am not only concerned about you, the Church, as a whole—I love the world too." *We haven't begun to be like Jesus until we love the world!* If anyone would understand, Jesus understands that it is hard to love the world sometimes because the world doesn't always present itself in a way that says, "Hey, I'm lovable." The truth is that the world usually comes across as hostile, irreverent, defiant, and anti-Christian.

Be that as it may, "For God so *loved the world* that He gave His only begotten Son..." (Jn. 3:16).

One of the things every human being must do to receive Jesus and reconciliation is to *repent*. Jesus went to great lengths to personally identify with us in repentance—even though He had nothing to repent about (see Mt. 3:13-15). Repentance is not one of those "screaming, slobbering, nose-running" words that we like to study in small groups. It doesn't give us goose bumps—it gives us soul lumps and sorrow fractures. The Bible says that "godly sorrow works repentance" (see 2 Cor. 7:10 KJV), but godly sorrow alone is not repentance. You can be really sorry and never change.

The Greek word for repentance, *metanoia*, is a combination of the preposition *meta*, which means "after," and the root verb *noieo*, which means "to consider, perceive, think, and understand."[2] Repentance is the act of reconsidering something while you are in the middle of it, and of then changing your actions and behavior accordingly. So if you repent, you stop going the direction you are going and you go a completely different direction.

God gave the Church some good news to tell people instead of some bad news. Why? Because He created us, and He knows that we respond to good news and positive communication a whole lot better than we do to bad news or negative words. When we see people going a certain direction and we say, "Hey, I've got some good news: *God is not mad at you!* He is not counting your sins against you," they will often *repent*, or reconsider where they are going and change directions. On the other hand, you can use my aunt's favorite news flash for unsaved people and say, "If you keep running down this road, you are going to hell at 72 heartbeats a minute." I don't know what you've found, but in my experience, most people who hear you say, "Don't go down to hell," will just look at you and say, "Who are you to tell me that? If I want to go to hell, I'm going." We have a built-in filter for bad news because there's so much of it. We ignore it, sometimes to our own hurt.

My wife Barbara and I were on a ride at Cedarpoint Amusement Park in Ohio one time when we came face-to-face with this side of human nature. The park had overhead cable cars that crossed over the park and we decided to save ourselves a walk and enjoy a nice view besides. When our cable car had crossed the park and stopped, Barb was the first to get up so she could leave the car. Just as she was stepping off the cable car, the ride attendant who held the door open said to us, "*Bump your head*" in a nice, professional tone. What did we do? We looked at him (with odd expressions on our faces) and *ducked*. I stopped and said, "Why did you say, 'Bump your head'?" He said, "Well, sir, we have been telling people for years, 'Watch your head,' and they *still* bump their heads." That's what the Church has been doing for years. We have been saying, singing, shouting, and preaching at the top of our lungs, "You are going to hell!" and they say, "Show us the way. We don't want to miss it." Then we have the unmitigated gall and audacity to say, "Yes, and that's the 'good news'." Can you fathom that? We need to learn that people don't pay attention to negative signs. Look at the ministry of Jesus—the only people He was hard on were the religious hypocrites who thought they were the only holy ones on the planet. Jesus was gentle with sinners and saints alike, and He wooed them to Himself with words of life, light, and love.

A man who was trying to find a friend's house for the first time stopped in front of a barrier with a large sign that said, "Bridge Out." He looked down at the directions his friend had given him and said, "I don't believe it. This guy didn't tell me the bridge was out. Now what do I do?" He sat there and watched as several cars went around the sign and traveled down the road until they were out of sight. Then he said to his wife, "Somebody must be pulling a gag," and he put the car in gear. His wife said, "So you are going to go down this road?" He answered, "Everybody else is," and drove around the barrier and went down the road. When he reached the point where the bridge was out, he saw another sign that was even bigger than the last one that said, "*I Told You the Bridge Was Out!*" There are some people who just don't care about your signs and your bad news—even if they're true.

So what does this "good news/bad news" situation have to do with us and God's "tribulator"? The Lord uses the "tribulator" to remove the chaff in our lives. By chaff, I'm referring to the things that are intertwined into our thinking and lifestyles that undermine our ability to model unity and reconciliation to others. This chaff has to be "beaten" off of us, and God does it day after day through adversity, challenges, correction, and special "assignments" to difficult people.

If you pray, "God, please send me someone to love," He will probably send you somebody who is a mess, and he'll show up just as soon as you finish that prayer. The Lord doesn't make it easy for us because He isn't interested in accumulating a crowd—He wants disciples who will be like Him. That's why God's Word is filled with difficult commands such as, "Love your enemy. If he's hungry, feed him. If he's thirsty, give him a drink" (see Lk. 6:27; Rom. 12:20). Most of us can't handle the idea that if we gather a thousand hungry people, feed them, and then give an altar call, that most of them will leave. So we try to do it *our way* and demand that conditions be met before offering people God's *unconditional* love. We preach a "hard word" of hellfire first and give an altar call, then feed the hardy few who are left.

## One Measure of Success

Look at what Jesus did: He *fed the multitude first* and *then* gave them the true word about God's love and the truth about hell. When most of the people left Him, Jesus didn't get upset. Why? Because He was more concerned with doing the will of His Father than with gathering the numbers and appearance of success. He only had one measure of success in life, and that was *doing what God wanted Him to do*.

As we begin to fulfill our call as ministers of reconciliation, we will also begin to experience the pain of rejection and the difficulty of ministering to the unlovely. This forces the chaff in our lives out into the open, and it gradually helps conform us to the image of our wonderful Savior who loves everyone without conditions or strings attached. This threshing process in our lives continues every day of our earthly existence, and we need to understand that it is a healthy and necessary part of our life in Christ. You should know by now that even though you repented of your sin and received Jesus as Lord and Savior on Sunday, you will also have to repent of certain sins on Monday. Although God did something wonderful in your life on Wednesday, He will have to do something in your life on Thursday and Friday as well. (No, I'm not saying that you have to get saved again— you just have to get wacked with the tribulator again and get some chaff knocked out of you.) The only reason God kicks our chickens is to help us discover that we can really walk and fly now. If He didn't love us enough to kick our chickens, then we would still be lying on our backs in our church buildings, clucking away contentedly like we were meant to spend life with our legs up in the air.

God wants us to prepare ourselves for the long haul. He is not going to kick all our chickens in one day. Sometimes we expect instant holiness and perfection just like we can pop a can of dough and bake instant biscuits in ten minutes. It is not going to happen that way. We seem to insist on approaching the Christian life in the same way as the Christian who prays, "God, I want patience, *and I want it now!*" No, the character of God comes in increments day by day. Somebody said that mental illness is contagious. You get it from your kids (and they find new ways to test your patience and endurance), from other Christians who don't always act in Christ-like ways, and from unsaved co-workers. How do you react when you feel a boot on your backside or the stroke of the tribulator on your life? You say, "Well, Lord, I guess You are beating some of the chaff off of me now, right?"

All of us come into God's Kingdom carrying a lot of baggage that just doesn't belong in our new home. "Here I am, Lord. Man, I'm glad to be in the Kingdom of God. I brought my pornographic magazines with me, and a little marijuana over there on the side (just in case I need to do some meditating), and I brought my Ouija board too in case things get slow and I need some direction." I know this is an extreme example, but you would be shocked at how many of us in the Body of Christ only discovered that the Ouija board game was bad news several years *after* we became Christians. Some people are really surprised to discover the Ouija board's connection to the occult, and they often say, "That is a really neat game." (So is Russian roulette—as long as you don't have bullets in any of the chambers of the pistol. The Ouija board is fully loaded and ready to kill.)

Once we are brought into the Kingdom of God, we learn that our first motivation is to "seek first the Kingdom of God" (see Mt. 6:33). From our first day on in God's family, the Lord begins to teach us how to hear His voice and obey—even when He asks us to do things that seem to be the opposite of what we think should be done. We think we should hate our enemies, but God tells us to love them. We want to curse them, but God commands us to pray for them. In anger, some people think that they should attack abortion clinics or members of other anti-Christian religions, but God says, "No, love them. Pray for them. Minister reconciliation to them. Tell them that I love them, and that I'm not counting their sins against them."

God wants us to change our attitude about each other and about the unsaved world. He wants us to take His love into the streets, into the workplace, and into our neighbors' homes. He wants us to be like Jesus. God's Word says:

*Therefore, holy brethren, partakers of a heavenly calling,* **consider Jesus**, *the Apostle and High Priest of our confession.* **He was faithful to Him who appointed Him...** (Hebrews 3:1-2).

Jesus Christ is utterly faithful. When Jesus looked at a large crowd of people—many of whom were only along for the ride—He "felt compassion for them because they were like sheep without a shepherd" (Mk. 6:34b). When you see people doing things that are peculiar to their nature and temperament as unregenerate people, *they don't need your disgust* (no matter how disgusting they are). They need your compassion. Can you recall a time in your life when you were lost?

There is an expression that says, "Lost men go in circles." People who get lost in a forest invariably end up walking in circles over and over again. Sometimes they have unknowingly come to within a half mile of a main road. People in the world are circling right now as we watch them. Meanwhile we are busily writing books about how dumb they look as they wander in their circles and how the masses of humanity are organized in rebellion toward God. The truth is that we were all that way. If we don't remember that we were a mess before God came into our lives, then every now and then He will pull back the curtain and play back some of the videos of our stupidity! Then He will remind us that the reason we are in the Kingdom today is because we have a great High Priest who is faithful, even in the middle of tribulations and trials.

The late Mother Theresa, the dedicated Roman Catholic nun who devoted almost 69 years of her life to Christian service, spent 50 of those years serving the millions of lower caste poor and lepers in Calcutta, India. I remember hearing about the time she ministered to a young man who had been lying so long on a street in Calcutta that part of the flesh from his back remained on the street when workers lifted his body from the pavement. He was obviously dying, and he stank. When he was brought into the Nirmal Hridayhim ("Pure Heart") Home for Dying Destitutes operated by Mother Theresa's Sisters of Charity, even the experienced people who normally cared for the destitute were revolted by the sight and smell of the man's physical state.

Mother Theresa came into the room and began to care for him personally. Those who saw it were amazed that she nourished and nurtured him as though he was going to live a hundred years. All this despite the fact that she knew that he was going to die no matter what she did—she had seen it countless times in the decades she had nursed the sick and dying. It didn't make any difference to her. She washed him and gently cared for him until he passed away in her arms that day. A witness to the incident said, "I asked Mother Theresa, 'How is it that you can continue to do that day after day after day, when there are so many millions of people that you know have died?' She said, *'God didn't call me to be successful. He called me to be faithful.'* "[3] These words are burned into my heart as I seek to be a faithful minister of reconciliation.

### Endnotes

1. *Merriam-Webster's Collegiate Dictionary*, 10th ed. (Springfield, Massachusetts; Merriam-Webster, Inc., 1994), 1260, *tribulation*.

2. James Strong, *Strong's Exhaustive Concordance of the Bible* (Peabody, Massachusetts: Hendrickson Publishers, n.d.), *repentance* (G3341, G3340, G3539).

3. I heard this story (including the reference to Mother Theresa) in a talk given at a National Prayer Breakfast in Washington, D.C. many years ago.

# Chapter 9

# Jesus Has Some Strange Kids

God is not limited by our limitations. Just because you do something in His name doesn't necessarily mean that God is in it with you! When I was a kid, the members of our church used to worship the Lord on the corner of Monroe and Clinton in Buffalo, New York. Our largest service would only draw about 100 people, but we thought *we were* the Church. Anyone outside of our sanctified little world wasn't saved, and we were quick to tell them so.

We knew that they weren't saved because they wore lipstick, did "things" to their hair, and wore dresses that came all the way up to just below their knees. We knew that they were doomed because the men wore colors and smoked. We were sure that we were saved, and we were equally sure that everyone else "was going to bust hell wide open and they were going there at 72 heartbeats a minute" (because that's what my aunt used to say).

Now the interesting thing I have found out since then is that even though God sent His Son into this world, He still stands outside our little private worlds. He doesn't come inside our worlds to settle in with us and say, "I believe the same thing you believe." Why? Because He knows better. He knows that there is at least one other group right across the street who feels the same way we feel (that they are "in" and we are "out"). Everywhere I go, I can find huge numbers of people who will raise their hands when I ask, "How many of you were in a church where you were told, 'This is the *only church*, and if you are going to go to Heaven, then you are going to have to go from *here*'?"

Sadly, that's the kind of reality people live with in much of the Church world today. We always expect God to come into our little hand-scrawled circle in the dirt, but God is saying, "Children, I gave you a bigger place than that. My world is larger than the universe, and it is certainly larger than you! It is larger, deeper, and broader than anything you have ever thought about. There are things in My world that you won't even get to see before you come to be with Me. There are truths, knowledge, facts, data, and levels of existence that you will never experience in your lifetime."

You can't know all that God knows, and you can't know everyone who is serving Him either. Like the prophet Elijah, we want to stay in our cave and bawl about being the only ones serving God, and He is shaking His wise head and saying, "I have yet 7,000 who have not yet bowed their knee—in your neighborhood alone!" (from my adaptation of Romans 11:4). I don't want to shock you, but we need to realize that God is using some people whom we wouldn't ever pick for our first-string religious team. Praise God. He doesn't need our permission, because one of His unlikely picks was Peter. Another one was Saul the Christian killer, and another one was *you*.

According to the Scriptures, God did some wonderfully strange things in the New Testament era. He came to the newly created Church composed of slaves and free men, rich and poor, wise and foolish, Jews and Gentiles, and males and females, and stirred them all together in His love. Then He put His hand upon unlearned fishermen, Jewish intellectuals, racially mixed teenagers, widows, men with criminal records (a necessary evil for early Church leaders), and even a *woman*—and He made them *apostles*! Can you believe that? Doesn't God know that you just don't make women apostles? Hasn't He heard the sermons?

Only wealthy, free, male, Jewish people can be apostles—how could God miss that basic, fundamental rule? He didn't miss anything—He chose whom He chose for His own glory and without our approval, without our input, and with no apologies to us. He must have been right. The Scriptures say, "Greet Andronicus and Junias, my kinsmen, and my fellow prisoners, who are *outstanding among the apostles*, who also were in Christ before me" (Rom. 16:7). Junias is a feminine Greek name, and she was probably married to Andronicus. Whether we like it or not, God can choose whoever He wants whenever He wants. If He wants to, He can choose a little kid and send him to bring you the word of the Lord. There is no distinction with Him.

*For you are all sons of God through faith in Christ Jesus. For all of you who were baptized into Christ have clothed yourselves with Christ. There is neither Jew nor Greek, there is neither slave nor free man, there is neither male nor female; for you are all one in Christ Jesus* (Galatians 3:26-28).

Paul taught that there is only one generic category for people who have been baptized in Christ: sons of God. Whether the Scriptures uses the terms "sons of God," "child of God," "children of God," or "saints," God is transcending gender distinctions to speak to the "spirit man" within all of us. When we read, "sons of God," we know that God is talking about male *and* female *offspring* of God. These terms aren't concerned with gender; they are concerned with an entire class of redeemed people.

Paul said, "For all of you who were baptized into Christ have clothed yourselves with Christ" (Gal. 3:27). Another way of saying that is, "If you were baptized *at all* into Christ, then you have clothed yourself in Christ." There is no way to be baptized into Christ and not "put on" or be clothed in Christ. This is one of the areas of the Christian life where you simply have no choice in the matter.

The Greek word for "baptized" is very interesting. "Baptize" is a transliteration, or a letter-by-letter spelling of the original Greek term *baptizo*, which means "to dip, to immerse, to submerge, to put under, to make fully wet." So when I am put into Christ, I am baptized into Christ. I am immersed, submerged, and inundated in His sphere, and "made fully wet" in the place called the Body of Christ.

When you and I were baptized "into Christ," we were literally moved into a supernatural environment that no longer honors the distinctions we used in society. Virtually every distinction that is considered appropriate for human society is inappropriate in the society of Jesus Christ. Society may say it is appropriate to divide people into groups by calling them "Jew or Greek," but not the Church. Society may differentiate between bond or free (meaning slave and free man). That division does not exist in Christ.

Now let me start meddling for a moment. In the case of gender divisions, the Western world is slightly ahead of the members of the Church! North America and most of the developed nations of Europe have made serious efforts to remove sex discrimination from the workplace, the schools, and government institutions. These efforts have been heavy-handed at times, and too weak at other times, but at least the problem of sex discrimination was recognized and addressed. The North American Church, on the other hand, has clung to the belief that women are second-class citizens in Church life—despite the clear teachings and ministry examples of Jesus and Paul the apostle.

In Paul's eyes, it was inappropriate to purposely divide the Body of Christ by calling them male or female. I am well aware of his teachings on marriage relationships and conduct in the Church, but he concludes with great force by saying: "There is neither Jew nor Greek, there is neither slave nor free man, there is neither male nor female; for you are all one in Christ Jesus" (Gal. 3:28).

In Christ, in this supernatural environment, there is neither Jew nor Greek (no race distinctions), bond or free (no economic or social distinctions), male or female (no gender distinctions). Outside of this, you are still who you are. If your hair was brown when you got saved, then you will still have brown hair (for a while at least) after you are saved. If you didn't have a lot of hair when you got saved, then you shouldn't expect to see a new crop of hair sprouting the morning after your conversion, for in Christ there is neither bald nor curly (according to the "Garlington Comic Relief Version" of the Bible). I had flat feet when I was born again and I can tell you with certainty that my feet are even flatter today. My friend, the distinctions that we cherish in human society are not distinctions that we cherish when we come into the Body of Christ.

## Twelve Distinctions Dividing the Church

*For there is **no distinction** between Jew and Greek; for the same Lord is Lord of all, abounding in riches for all who call upon Him; for "WHOEVER WILL CALL UPON THE NAME OF THE LORD WILL BE SAVED"* (Romans 10:12-13).

I've found a number of distinctions in Scripture that are obliterated when you and I are baptized into Christ. These are all distinctions, or fleshly factors, that unnaturally divide the Body of Christ when we allow them to:

1. Racial distinctions

2. Cultural distinctions

3. National distinctions

4. Gender distinctions

5. Economic distinctions

6. Class (or social) distinctions

7. Religious distinctions

8. "Singleness" distinction

9. Divorce distinction

10. AIDS distinction

11. Political distinctions

12. Educational distinctions

Paul told us under divine authority that there are *no distinctions* between us in God's eyes. The only reason we can stand before Him is because His Son, Jesus Christ, personally paid the price for our freedom and washed us in His blood. Period. Everything beyond that is stuff that belongs in God's "damned trash can," where you will find Paul's impeccable racial bloodline and fancy theological schooling as well as Peter's temper and racial prejudice.

### There Is One Race in God's Kingdom

The greatest racial conflict of Paul's day was the ancient hatred between Jews and Gentiles (the Gentiles are typified in the New Testament by the Greeks). Yet Paul said, "For there is no distinction between Jew and Greek; for the same Lord is Lord of all…" (Rom. 10:12). So if you are black and you call on the name of the Lord, He will hear you. If you are a white female and you call on Him, He will hear you. If you are an 80-year-old Japanese horticulturist and you call on Him, He will hear you. If you are the child of a Japanese-Polish American, He will hear you (and enjoy your unique accent). There are no distinctions in His presence. He will hear you whether you are a millionaire, an IRS agent, an Afghan rebel, or a Brazilian coffee grower.

If you call upon His name, He will hear you. There are no distinctions in His house. Does this mean that we are not different from each other? Absolutely not. God loves variety—He invented it. What it does mean is that we all have the same value and standing in His eyes, much like seven very different children in one family are each dearly and equally loved by their earthly parents. We are all of one race and blood in God's house:

> And hath made **of one blood** all nations of men for to dwell on all the face of the earth, and hath determined the times before appointed, and the bounds of their habitation; that they should seek the Lord...for in Him we live, and move, and have our being; as certain also of your own poets have said, **For we are also His offspring** (Acts 17:26-28 KJV).

Paul gave the believers in Corinth some very interesting instructions in First Corinthians: "But as God hath distributed to every man, as the Lord hath called every one, so let him walk. And so I ordain in all churches" (1 Cor. 7:17 KJV). What is he talking about? Aren't all distinctions removed when we are "in Christ"?

The Bible says the race of mankind was created in the image of God (see Gen. 1:26). Jesus said that God is a Spirit in John 4:24, so what are we in our essential creation? Spirit. We are spirit people, and the Bible tells us that we have no business knowing and relating to one another according to the outer appearance and limitations of our fleshly bodies. We are spirit beings created in God's image. It just so happens that some of us come out one way and some of us another way in terms of the "outer covering" that we need to exist in a world of physical matter, with its built-in time and space limitations. I like what Bill Gillams calls it. He says that we all have "an earth suit" that can relate to the environment we are in. Unfortunately, we are so silly that we insist on categorizing ourselves by the color, shape, and different features of our earth suits instead of by the genuine article inside.

The day I was born, the doctor came to the door and said to an African-American man named John Wesley Garlington, Sr., "It's a boy." From my first entrance into this world, one of my callings in our society was to be an African-American male. I didn't do anything to "deserve it" or to be "stuck with it." That was my calling in life. I also received other callings as I went down the road of life. But when I was baptized into Christ, I was called to be a son of God and an heir of all the promises of God by faith. I was called to be conformed to the image of Jesus Christ, and little else mattered from that point on *in comparison to* my high call in Christ.

> *For even as the body is one and yet has many members, and all the members of the body, though they are many, are one body, so also is Christ. For by one Spirit we were all baptized into one body, whether Jews or Greeks, whether slaves or free, and we were all made to drink of one Spirit* (1 Corinthians 12:12-13).

Here is the sad news (for some): The radical black activist who receives Jesus as Lord and Savior is in for a shock when he meets the radical skinhead who also came to Jesus. They don't realize it, but they have both been baptized into the *same body*. Even before they get up off their knees and open their eyes, they were instantly transformed into "two seeds in the same watermelon." They are blood brothers for eternity, whether they like it or not.

## We Share a Common Kingdom Culture

Large families who gather for family reunions think nothing of the different cultures they experience in different

states, cities, and regions of the world. The brother from Los
Angeles has no problem relating to his younger sister who
lives in New Bedford, Massachusetts. Uncle Bob from Kla-
math Falls, Oregon, can talk by the hour with Buford, his
second cousin who hitched a ride to the reunion from his
home in Houma, Louisiana. The really shocking discovery is
that all of them can relate to Aunt Maude and Uncle Hubert
from Brooklyn, New York. Their resident cultures are different, but their family roots and bloodline are the same. They
share the same memories and language of a common source.
So it is with everyone who has been baptized by one Spirit
into one Lord and Savior. Our resident cultures as African-
Americans, Irish Americans, French Canadians, or Norwe-
gian Minnesotans take a distant second place behind our
common bloodline and identity as royal sons and daughters
of God.

We need to relax and take joy in the fact that the Holy
Spirit freely chooses to manifest Himself in rap music, in
Hip Hop, in classical pieces by Bach and Beethoven, in rock
'n' roll, and in traditional gospel. His presence can be manifested through any life and gift surrendered to Christ. The
differences that society majors on still exist, but they simply
no longer matter! In Christ, they become signposts of God's
power and glory in unity with diversity instead of beacons of
division.

### One Nation From Many Nations

*But you are A CHOSEN RACE, A royal PRIESTHOOD,*
***A HOLY NATION***, *A PEOPLE FOR God's OWN POS-*
*SESSION, that you may proclaim the excellencies of Him*
*who has called you out of darkness into His marvelous*
*light; for you once were NOT A PEOPLE, but **now you are***
***THE PEOPLE OF GOD**... (1 Peter 2:9-10).*

We don't seem to understand that the Holy Spirit doesn't
have a "black church" or a "white church" any more than He

has a Korean church or an accountant church. We all belong
to Christ's Church, and we are called to model on earth what
already exists in Heaven. What exists in Heaven? John has to
describe the scene in technicolor: "After these things I
looked, and behold, a great multitude, which no one could
count, from *every nation* and *all tribes* and *peoples* and *tongues*,
standing before the throne and before the Lamb, clothed in
white robes..." (Rev. 7:9).

You and I are praying that this reality will come to earth
every time we pray the prayer Jesus taught us to pray in the
Gospels, "...Thy will be done, *on earth* as it is in heaven" (Mt.
6:10). Do we know what we are actually praying when we say
this? We are saying, "*Lord, get rid of or change every church that
doesn't have a rainbow*"! God loves to mix His colors into a
brilliant portrait of unity and harmony in the love and grace
of Jesus. Sometimes we don't want to mix with other colors,
cultures, and nationalities, but God says, "That's an order.
The love of Christ compels you." He tells us, "Just love them
or I'll get someone to kick your chicken."

### The Extinction of Religious Distinctions

Two of the most obvious and unyielding religious distinctions of Paul's day were circumcision and dietary laws. Yet
Paul dared to declare by the Spirit:

> *Was any man called already circumcised? Let him not be-
> come uncircumcised. Has anyone been called in uncircum-
> cision? Let him not be circumcised. Circumcision is nothing,
> and uncircumcision is nothing, but what matters is the
> keeping of the commandments of God. Let each man remain
> in that condition in which he was called* (1 Corinthians
> 7:18-20).

When Paul told his fellow Jews that circumcision was nothing, he was risking his neck to tell them that centuries of religious distinctions meant nothing once Christ died on the cross
and rose again. "Well, they drink *wine* for communion—the

kind that has alcohol in it." *Is that the only reason you don't fellowship with them?* "Well, the Bible says, 'Wine is a mocker, strong drink a brawler, and whoever is intoxicated by it is not wise' " (righteously quoted from Proverbs 20:1). *Do you think they can get drunk on that little bit?* "I don't want to risk anything." *Why don't you fellowship with that church?* "Well, they believe that the saints are going to go through the tribulation and I just don't believe it myself." *It's great to believe that you won't go through the tribulation, but what if you do? Don't you think it would be good to know what they teach "just in case"?*

Christians allow themselves to be divided over some of the most trivial things! Remember that it wasn't your views about communion that got you in the Church. It wasn't your amillennial, premillennial, postmillennium, or pan-millennium convictions that washed away your sins and won you the title of son of God. Perhaps we should all be "pan-millennialists" and walk in faith that it will all pan out all right no matter what goes on! No, we insist on reaching through the bars of our cage to rattle the identical cage of the guy next to us, saying, "Why don't you come out of that little cage and come into mine?" Paul, though, tells us to live as we were called.

*Why don't you fellowship with those people?* "Well, they eat collard greens and sweet potato pies." "I just can't sit in public with anybody who talks with that kind of accent and wears those strange clothes." "They're from the wrong side of town." "I just can't relate to people from the South." "My family has avoided touching Republicans for 70 years. I ain't about to begin now."

We've all been baptized into one Body of Christ and we get this most glorious of all cultures. I'm not talking about a "melting pot," because there is something precious about our diversity that God wants to keep. He is putting together a divine mosaic that gives Him glory and pleasure. What do you do about the elderly? Love them. How about the kids?

Become like them. How about the people with AIDS? Make them a real part of the church. How about the folks who are struggling with their identity and their sexual confusion? Love them and find a ministry for them. How about the singles? Singles just need to know that God loves them and that we love them—the way they are. And the rest of the church shouldn't impose marriage on them if they don't want to be married (but yes, they need to stay celibate if they don't want to be married). We are a living mosaic where there are very clear identities and clear contributions with diversities that we can appreciate. In Christ, diversity is our strength. It causes us to be an expression of God's grace, mercy, and riches. We are a miracle of God in a very divided world.

### "I Are Edjumacated"

There is only one culture—the culture of the Kingdom. What happens when you come into the Kingdom of God? You enter through the same door as everyone else, whether they knock at the door with a Ph.D., a GED, or BVDs in their hand. Does your lack of education cause you to feel inferior at times? I know people who don't have a high school diploma and I also know people who have them. Frankly, there are times when I would rather fellowship with the folks who don't have a diploma because they're sometimes more "real" and sincere. It isn't just a question of how much education you have (or as one brother said, "edjumacation"). The real issue is whether or not you can hear from God. If you can hear from God, then I want to talk to you. If you can't hear from God, and you insist on coming to me and saying, "I want to share with you about the ineluctable modality of the visible as it relates to the lack of humility and the whole of humankind—anthropology and sociology notwithstanding," then I'm not interested.

Sonship in Christ is the great equalizer. Again, Paul told the Galatians:

*For you are all sons of God through faith in Christ Jesus. For all of you who were baptized into Christ have clothed yourselves with Christ.* [Therefore, in Christ there] *is neither Jew nor Greek, there is neither slave nor free man, there is neither male nor female; for you are all one in Christ Jesus* (Galatians 3:26-28).

I believe Paul wrote this under the inspiration of the Holy Spirit to directly confront the traditional Jewish prayer that I understand had been prayed by Jewish men for countless generations in his day: "Lord, I thank You that You didn't make me a Gentile, a slave, or a woman."[1] (I trust they are not praying it now.)

Now, a lot of folks when they come through the door of the church check their brains. That's not good. You don't have to check your brains at the doorstep to the Body of Christ. You can keep your brains.

*For He Himself is our peace, who made both groups* [Jews and Gentiles] *into one, and broke down the barrier of the dividing wall, by abolishing in His flesh the enmity, which is the Law of commandments contained in ordinances, that in Himself He might make the two into one new man, thus establishing peace, and might reconcile them both **in one body*** [the Church] *to God through the cross, by it having put to death the enmity* (Ephesians 2:14-16).

In Scripture there are only three distinctions that we are specially called upon to deal with: Jew, Gentile, and the Church of God. There is enmity between Jew and Gentile. It is a spiritual condition. If there is enmity (bitter hatred, resentment, or malice) between your race and another race, I can assure you that it is spiritual enmity. There is another enmity that comes into play the moment you become a born-again Christian. If you get saved today and go home and sit across the table from your unsaved husband, you discover that there is a spiritual division between you. You are now spiritual enemies. You may not like it, but that's a reality for many people. That is one of the reasons why the Bible warns us not to be "unequally yoked" together with unbelievers, no matter how "nice" they are (see 2 Cor. 6:14 KJV).

The message of reconciliation begins at the communion table where we begin to say to one another, "We be brethren" (Gen. 13:8b KJV). That's from the King James Bible, not from the housing projects. We be brothers. My brothers and I fought at times, but I couldn't disassociate myself from them because we were immersed in the same family named Garlington.

There are distinctions in the Body of Christ that we need to recognize simply because they exist. It is a fact that some people in the Body of Christ have blue eyes, and some even have green eyes or hazel eyes. But we can no longer afford to be separated from somebody because of some kind of weird difference that no one but God has control over anyway! None of us can add to our height or change our basic body characteristics, and none of us was able to choose our parents or economic status at birth. We all *were* given a choice about Jesus Christ, however. Once we make that choice, we are on level playing ground in Christ.

## Does God Have to Reconcile *Everyone*?

What's God up to anyway? He is reconciling all things in Heaven and on earth. The problem comes with that phrase, "all things." If you haven't noticed it yet, God has some strange kids. Have you noticed that He sometimes gives special gifts to certain people who also happen to have really obnoxious personalities? If it wasn't for the gift, you wouldn't put up with those jokers for one more minute! They are obnoxious with a capital "O." People will say, "Man, isn't that person obnoxious?" "Yes, *he is really talented.*" It seems to me that the Holy Spirit does this to leverage or maneuver us into character-building situations that we would normally take great pains to avoid.

Let's face it: There are some people whose personalities are not going to change this side of Heaven. I know a very interesting, creative, and talented person who was born with what has to be a master's degree in "obnoxiouscation." For some reason, God decided that my wife and I had to learn how to love this individual. We obediently invited this person to our house for dinner one day. Barbara had set the table very beautifully and just as she was about to serve the food, this unique person decided that he wanted to blow his nose. My wife watched in shock as he took one of her fine linen napkins from the table and lifted it to his nose...it was just too much for her. Barbara screamed his name out loud and stopped the progress of that fine linen toward that equally fine proboscis. He looked at her with an incredibly innocent and blank look and said, "Oh, you mean this isn't acceptable here?" Obnoxious and gifted.

Repeat these words to yourself exactly as I've written them here: *Jesus has some strange kids.* You may be tempted to mutter under your breath so I can't hear you, "And I'm glad I'm not one of them," but it is my duty to tell you, "Yes, you are." (Don't stop reading now. There's hope.)

God is out to reconcile all things to Himself in Heaven and in earth. When I first came to Christ, I had some hang-ups. As I continued to walk with Him, I still had some hang-ups. I have to admit that as I write these words, I still have a few hang-ups. (If you ask Barbara, she might expand or expound on my statement, so don't ask her.) Somebody said it like this: "He was hung up for my hang-ups." Aren't we all glad for that? We need to understand that *it really was God* in Christ reconciling the world to Himself and that it is God in you who is reconciling the world to Himself. People need to be able to come up to you and say, "I rejoice in the Christ that is in you." We need to exemplify Christ through our lives.

You and I are in the same body and we have the same Father and the same mother. I can't hurt you without hurting myself, and I can't bless you without blessing myself. I can't reject you without rejecting myself. Since Paul makes this clear in First Corinthians 12:21, then I want to say to you as clearly as I can: "*I have need of thee.*" By now we should have a pretty good idea about which way to answer God's constant question, "Do you want to be *right*, or *reconciled*?"

### Endnote

1. From "Early Morning Prayer" in *The Orthodox Jewish Prayer Book*, or *Siddur*.

# Chapter 10

# Kill Your Father's Bull

I remember reading a story in a book of sermon illustrations about a prison chaplain in nineteenth century England. This chaplain was required by the law to read to condemned men a long string of Scriptures describing the perils of eternal damnation that would follow people who did not give their lives to the Lord. The chaplain was taken to a prisoner's cell to accompany him to the gallows, and he began to read about all the aspects of burning in hell for eternity "where the worm does not die" and so on (see Mk. 9:44). When the guards finally escorted the chaplain and the condemned man to the place where the execution was to take place, the prisoner turned, looked at the clergyman, and said, "Sir, if I believed one thing that you read to me today—if I believed there was any truth in it at all—I would crawl *across England on my hands and knees through glass and through bricks and through metal to save one person from what you just described.*"

*Do you really believe that people will end up in a hell without God?* As members of the only agency in society authorized to offer a solution, we don't have a choice: *We must model unity*. The writer of Hebrews said, "Since then we have a great high priest who has passed through the heavens, Jesus the Son of God, *let us hold fast our confession*" (Heb. 4:14).

The only reason he would say this is because he knew by the Spirit that we would be tempted to let go of our confession because of discouragement, fear, or selfishness (just to name a few possibilities). What do we do with the message of reconciliation? One thing is sure: We can't bury it!

In the apostle Paul's second letter to the church at Corinth, he described how Christians aren't fighting against flesh and blood. He said that they aren't fighting with mere human weapons, but with "divine power to demolish strongholds" (2 Cor. 10:4 NIV). After he talks about taking every disobedient thought captive, Paul says something that I believe is a principle in God's Kingdom: "And we are ready to punish all disobedience, *whenever your obedience* is complete" (2 Cor. 10:6).

This means that God didn't promise to deal with our enemies (in the spirit realm and otherwise) no matter what we do and how we live. There are clear conditions to the promise. (God is no fool.) God is saying, "If you don't keep your act together, then I won't deal with your enemies. In fact, I will use your enemies to deal with you!" If you doubt that, just read a few pages from the Books of Exodus, Judges, or First Kings. Read through the prophetic books and see how God used Israel's enemies to deal with her disobedience.

Why should the Church be any different? Has God changed? Why would we think that He would tolerate disobedience in our day any more than He did in Moses' day? A lot of what we see going on in the Church and around us isn't the result of satan running loose—it's a result of *our own failure to obey God*. When we refuse to obey God, it is pointless for us to quote Scriptures as positive confessions. The most powerful confession that a Christian can have is the Lord's statement, "Well done, good and faithful servant! You have been faithful..." (Mt. 25:21 NIV).

## God Calls Closet Cowards

You and I have a decision to make. Do you remember an Old Testament figure named Gideon? If you remember him as a "mighty man of valor," you are right to do so. If you think that he was always the brave hero type, then you are wrong.

*Then the angel of the Lord came and sat under the oak that was in Ophrah, which belonged to Joash the Abiezrite as his son Gideon was beating out wheat in the wine press in order to save it from the Midianites. And the angel of the Lord appeared to him and said to him, "The Lord is with you, O valiant warrior"* (Judges 6:11-12).

Sounds pretty impressive, doesn't it? At first glance, this sounds like one of those impressive angelic visitations to a mighty man of faith and power of Bible legend. It isn't. Look a little closer. Why was our mighty man of faith and power threshing wheat in "the winepress"? According to John C.H. Laughlin, as quoted in *The Holman Bible Dictionary*, "In Old Testament times the presses for making wine were usually cut or hewed out of rock (Isa. 5:2)."[1] In other words, mighty Gideon was threshing wheat out of sight so the mean Midianites wouldn't steal the family's harvest. (He was hiding in a hole.)

Now, there isn't much evidence of Gideon's bravery at this point. He was really acting a bit more like a coward. Look at what the angel of the Lord said to this closet coward: "The Lord is with you, O valiant warrior" (Judg. 6:12). When Gideon the not-so-valiant heard the angel say, "valiant warrior," I think he said, "Who, me?" Then he launched into a series of questions that were really accusations against God!

*Then Gideon said to him, "O my lord, if the Lord is with us, why then has all this happened to us? And where are all His miracles which our fathers told us about, saying, 'Did not the Lord bring us up from Egypt?' But now the Lord has*

*abandoned us and given us into the hand of Midian"*
(Judges 6:13).

After Gideon asked the Lord these insulting "why me"
and "why us" questions, the Lord overlooked his words and
the angel said, "Go in this your strength and deliver Israel
from the hand of Midian. Have I not sent you?" (Judg. 6:14b)
Look at Gideon's answer in verse 15: "O Lord, how shall I
deliver Israel? Behold, my family is the least in Manasseh,
and I am the youngest in my father's house" (Judg. 6:15b).
Gideon said the same thing most of us say when God shows
us a glimpse of our destiny: "I can't do it." He had the same
problem many of us have today: He had a *poor self-image.*
God didn't buy it—He called Gideon a warrior anyway because He knew Gideon's divine destiny. The same is true for
you: *Your background has nothing to do with God's choice of you.*
The Bible tells us that God uses dysfunctional people to save
the world (see 1 Cor. 1:26-29).

### Will You Take Your Father's Bull?

The Lord told Gideon that he had to do three things to
begin to fulfill God's prophetic plan for his life.

*Now the same night it came about that the Lord said to him,
"**Take your father's bull** and a second bull seven years old,
and **pull down the altar of Baal which belongs to your father**, and cut down the Asherah that is beside it; **and build
an altar to the Lord your God on the top of this stronghold** in an orderly manner, and take a second bull and offer
a burnt offering with the wood of the Asherah which you
shall cut down"* (Judges 6:25-26).

God ordered Gideon to tear down his father's altar to
Baal! Gideon's father had taught his son some evil traditions
that were going to separate him from his inheritance in Abraham if they weren't dealt with. Many fathers teach their children some ungodly traditions that are deadly. Some dads
build altars to the family tradition of racial prejudice. Others

build altars to the blind pursuit of money at all cost. Still others built altars to the persistant pursuit of sexual pleasure or alcoholic bliss—while their children watched. All of it has to go. Any altar, any tradition, any idea or value that is contrary to God's Word and character *must be torn down*.

God also told Gideon to *kill his father's bull*. How much of what your father told you amounts to a "load of bull" (things that are untrue, things that should be buried as waste)? I want to suggest to you that all of us are victims of our fathers' altars. (We don't have to show disrespect toward our natural fathers to separate the truth from the falsehoods in the things they taught and demonstrated to us. That is not what God is urging us to do.) What we believe about other people for the most part is what we have learned in our family setting. Don't expect to go out and save the world when you haven't done something with your father's altar and your father's bull.

Have you torn down your father's altars to prejudice and damaging stereotypes? Have you dismantled and destroyed every stone of division between races, nations, and sexes used on that altar? Are you prepared to kill your father's bull forever? Then begin to build a new altar in your life, an altar of obedience and commitment to the ministry of reconciliation. Start spreading the *good news* throughout your world instead of the "Midianite blues."

### Did the GIs Have Tails?

If you are white or a non-black race, think about what you heard about black folks in your family circles and history classes. How has this "altar" altered or skewed your view of African-Americans? (Hang on, I'm going to step on some black toes too in just a moment.) History reveals some interesting "altars" concerning some of the African-American GIs involved in the invasion and ultimate occupation of Nazi Germany during World War II. Many of these soldiers remember that when they patrolled the streets of Berlin, anytime they turned around, they would see people staring at them in an odd way. They found out that the German people, particularly the youth in the German schools, had been told by the Nazi propaganda machine that "black people had tails"!

In the same way, many Germans actually believed that Jews, blacks, and many of the Slavic people of Europe were intellectually inferior. That idea wasn't exclusively a German problem dating from the 1940's. Some Americans still believe that black people in general have lower intelligence quotients than the general population, even though scientific studies conclusively destroyed that myth decades ago.

All of us have to deal with "false altars" that our fathers built in our lives (even the best of fathers can pass along some bad ideas from time to time). A well-known American sportscaster lost his job in recent years because he broadcast a verbal slur based on a false stereotype concerning African-American athletes, and prominent leaders of all colors and races are finding themselves confronted by the harmful things coming from their mouths in public places.

### Tripped Up by a Rhyme

When I was a little boy, my father taught me a fun little rhyme that we used to use when picking sides for games or making simple choices. It went something like this: "Eenie, meenie, minie, moe, catch a tiger by the toe." I used this little innocent rhyme for 13 years, but one day I found myself in "the wrong neighborhood" and I heard some little kids saying the same little rhyme with a wicked little twist: "Eenie, meenie, minie, moe, catch a *nigger* by the toe." So much for my innocent memory. Yet those little children were *not* directing that new, racially slanted rhyme at me; they were probably reciting in all innocence what they had been taught by people they trusted and respected.

In the African-American community, you will find equally slanted viewpoints and statements being passed on to the children. I lived with black folks who had a problem with white folks, so in all their speech, white folks were "crackers." The reason this kind of stuff goes on is because we all seem to cherish exaggerated ideas about our importance. Outside of the lordship of Jesus, we think that we need to pull down other people so we can be lifted up. Now that's a devilish idea if I ever heard one.

I grew up in a black community where one of the cherished myths we were taught to believe was that "there wasn't a white man anywhere that could beat a black man in a fight." I took that myth with me to Lafayette High School in the heart of an Italian neighborhood in Buffalo, New York. Since I was a "negro" and proud of it ("African-American" and "black" weren't the politically correct terms back then), and since everybody obviously knew that "there wasn't a white man anywhere that could beat a black man in a fight," I walked into the locker room that day with a bold swagger and promptly bumped into an Italian boy who was just a little shorter than I was. I didn't apologize and neither did he.

Evidently this particular fellow hadn't heard that myth about "whiteys," because he just grabbed me by the throat and said, "I will kill you." The Holy Spirit spoke to me in that moment and said, "He will!" As for me, I was pleading the blood and trying to agree with my adversary quickly. I thought to myself, *If he ever lets me go, I'll never think that thought again!* Obviously, I was "myth-taken"!

## Going to See Miss Anne and Mr. Charlie

Evidently Rocky Marciano did not believe the stereotype that any black man could beat any white man either. At least you wouldn't be able to convince Joe Walcott that it's true. Are you with me? We deal with stereotypes all the time. "Black people can jump higher" (stereotype). I used to think that my mother and every woman in the black community worked for the *same white lady*, Miss Anne. They did, in a way.

I'd ask my mother, "Where are you going, Mom?" "I'm going to take care of Miss Anne's house." I'd ask my aunt the same thing and, to my surprise, she was going to Miss Anne's too. My friends said their moms were also going to Miss Anne's. We all thought that Miss Anne either had a really dirty house that needed a lot of cleaning or else she had a mighty clean house because everyone we knew worked for her. Then we noticed that they all went in different directions and began to realize that "Miss Anne" was the stereotypical name that black folks called every white woman who paid a black person to clean her house. It didn't take long for us to figure out why so many of the black men worked for "Mr. Charlie" after that. They were all stereotypes.

Barbara and I visited South Africa before the government there struck down that nation's official government policy of mandatory racial segregation. When we returned, people in the States asked us, "Was it bad there?" We said, "Yes, it was bad, but we saw something else there—something good—that we didn't see here." Dr. Martin Luther King, Jr., said, "The eleven o'clock hour [on Sunday] is the most segregated hour in all of the church" in America. But in South Africa we saw more white churches with persons of color attending them than we ever saw in the United States in those days! Now that was significant to me.

We are on very shaky ground when our politicians say to South Africans, "Why can't you all get your act together?" Why? Because they look at us and say, "Do you mean like you have your act together in Mississippi, and Alabama, and in Boston? Or do you mean like you have your American 'racial unity' act together in Brooklyn? Is that the way you have your act together?"

## Does He *Have* to Do It *Here*?

Meanwhile, large segments of the American Church are saying, "Well, any time now Jesus is going to come and get us out of this, and it will all be straightened out when we get to Heaven." I'm sorry to disappoint anyone or mess up anybody's theology, but *He's going to straighten it out now.* According to the Bible, God fully intends to display His manifold wisdom *through* His Church right in front of the world and the devil's armies (see Eph. 3:10 NIV).

God knows that we are all affected by our fathers' altars, even though we don't realize the degree to which they affect us. Even "significantly mature spiritual people" in close covenant relationships with you who belong to a different race or social class than you may slip up every now and then. I remember the time I was with a prominent figure in the nation. My friend and I were standing alongside one another after he had just finished his work on an extremely difficult project. He looked at me and said without thinking, "Man, I've been working just like a nigger." I thought to myself, *He doesn't even realize that he's talking to a "nigger."*

It was incredible to see how ingrained that particular racial slur has become in our society, despite our recent fascination with "political correctness" and ethnic sensitivity. The interesting thing is that even black folk say it about themselves once in a while. These are the kinds of things that God calls "our fathers' altars," and we've got to tear them down before we can get on with the purpose of God in our lives.

You've got to do it, no matter what ethnic group you belong to or what your skin color is. You have to look at your father's altar and say, "It's coming down." Even if you have to do it in the middle of the night like our mighty man of valor, Gideon, you had better do it. Frankly, some of us have learned some things from our parents that are just sheer "bull." If you've been in Jesus long enough, you are discovering that there are some wonderful people who just happen to be white, and that there are also some wonderful people who just happen to be black. You have probably noticed that there are also some really mean people who just happen to be black, and there are also some really mean people who just happen to be white. Their meanness doesn't stem from the color of their skin. It's the product of their sin and fallenness.

When people are constantly reminded that they are different from (and considered of less value than) the people around them, it will build a deep distrust in them. I went to a Bible college, a fundamental Bible college, that had a grand total of five black students in the student body. Everyone was very amicable to me in the school during classes, but when they were outside the school they wouldn't even speak to me. If they saw me on the street and didn't recognize me immediately, they would pass right on by without so much as a smile or a nod. Now it's easy to get an "attitude" when this happens. I immediately began to judge their Christianity rather than their failure to allow the Holy Spirit to do a redeeming work in their whole life.

### Just a White Folks Lover

One of my major challenges is to talk to black folks who are telling me, "The 'man' did this, and the 'man' did that, and 'those whiteys' are all alike." When I tell them, "It's not true, it really isn't true," they say, "Oh, you are just a white folks lover." Well, that's true. I tell them, "I do love white folks, and if you want to stone me for that, you can. But I love black folks too. What I'm learning to do is love *people*." I have a friend named Jackson Khosa who is a black pastor in South Africa. He looked straight at me one day and said, "Pastor Joseph, God didn't save me because I was black, but because I was a sinner."

Now how does that Bible passage go? "For God so loved *black folks*..."? "For God so loved *white folks*..."? "For God so loved *the world*..." (Jn. 3:16). I always found it odd that people like to make fun of the way "different" people speak English. I've noticed that East Indian people find it difficult to pronounce the letter "r" without rolling it. Chinese and Japanese people don't use the letter "l" in their alphabetic systems, so they have a hard time with the "l's" in the English language. The word *vanilla* will generally be pronounced "vanirra," and *chocolate* would become "chocarate." We don't want to recognize the simple fact that the historic speech patterns in their native languages predispose them to mispronounce certain words in the English language.

## Somebody Has to Lead

Now in the black community we have trouble with the "th" sound because it was not normally present in most African dialects. As a result, our ancestors who were brought to America from Africa against their will generally couldn't pronounce the "th" as they learned to speak English. This has been passed on along with the language modifications they came up with. The "th" sound on the end of a word like *with* becomes an "f" sound, and we say, "I'm going wif you." We're not stupid; we're trying to overcome several hundred years of intense training and predisposition. If the "th" is at the front of a word, we put a "d" there. We don't say "this"; we say "dis" and "dat"—even when we have a Ph.D. in literature or philosophy—much as a German person would pronounce "w" as a "v" in English pronunciations. Whether we pronounce the words correctly or not, somebody has to take the lead in tearing down these unholy altars of prejudice, hatred, division, and racism. Somebody has to step to the front and lead God's people in prayers of *repentance* for our wrongdoing toward one another (or for the wrongs done by those who lived before us). Isaiah the prophet tells us why:

> *For thus the Lord God, the Holy One of Israel, has said, "**In repentance** and rest you shall be saved, in quietness and*

*trust is your strength."* But *you were not willing* (Isaiah 30:15).

Here is the issue that God puts before us as ministers of reconciliation: Do we need to repent for our racism or for our families' racism? I believe that God is asking each one of us to tear down some ungodly altars from the past. This is a demand placed on every believer, regardless of color, ethnicity, culture, or racial history. When the prophet Daniel was interceding and standing in the gap for his nation, he realized that there was some sin that hadn't been dealt with in the purpose of God. He began to pray, "We have sinned, committed iniquity, acted wickedly, and rebelled, even turning aside from Thy commandments and ordinances" (Dan. 9:5). Now, the record shows that Daniel himself was a righteous person, so why was he repenting for acting wickedly and rebelling? *Daniel was taking spiritual initiative and personal responsibility for the sinful actions of his people.* Perhaps you and I should do the same. Maybe we have come to the Kingdom for just such a time as this.

It doesn't make any difference what color you are if you are part of the Body of Christ. The reality is this: The Bible says, "But if you bite and devour one another, take care lest you be consumed by one another" (Gal. 5:15). Somebody in the Body of Christ has to take some initiative for reconciliation, and that "somebody" is you and me.

### The Cold Within

Six humans trapped by happenstance
In black and bitter cold,
Each one possessed a stick of wood
Or so the story's told.

Their dying fire in need of logs
The first woman held hers back,

For on the faces around the fire
She noticed one was black.

The next man looking across the way
Saw one not of his church,
And couldn't bring himself to give
The fire his stick of birch.

The third one sat in tattered clothes
He gave his coat a hitch,
Why should his log be put to use
To warm the idle rich.

The rich man just sat back and thought
Of the wealth he had in store,
And how to keep what he had earned
From the lazy, shiftless poor.

The black man's face bespoke revenge
As the fire passed from his sight,
For all he saw in his stick of wood
Was a chance to spite the white.

And the last man of this forlorn group
Did naught except for gain,
Giving only to those who gave
Was how he played the game.

The logs held tight in death's still hands
Was proof of human sin,
They didn't die from the cold without
They died from the cold within.[2]

Do you have any altars that need to be torn down in your life? Tear it down right now in the name of Jesus Christ. Have you killed your father's bull and sacrificed it to God? Have you built a new altar with stones of obedience and reconciliation from your own life? Now is the time; today is the day to begin anew.

## Endnotes

1. John C.H. Laughlin, Ph.D., as quoted in *The Holman Bible Dictionary*, Trent C. Butler, gen. ed. (Nashville: Holman Bible Publishers, 1991), under the topic, "winepress."

2. Author unknown.

# Chapter 11

# The Cross and a Curse Gone Astray

On the day Jesus Christ was crucified by Roman soldiers under the approving eyes of Jewish leaders while other Jews and Gentiles who loved Him wept, something else happened that shouldn't have—at least according to some folks.

*And as they were coming out, they found a man of Cyrene named Simon, whom they pressed into service to bear His cross* (Matthew 27:32).

Simon was a native of Cyrene, a Libyan city near the coast of North Africa that was settled by Greek colonists in the seventh century B.C. It was the chief city of the Roman province of Cyrenaica.[1] For some reason, God chose an African man (perhaps a Jewish convert) to be at the wrong place at the wrong time when the Roman soldiers escorting Jesus decided to press someone into service to carry the cross. (They wouldn't do this to a Roman citizen.) This African man, Simon, was probably the last friendly (or at least non-hostile) human being to touch Jesus before He died on the cross.

"It shouldn't have been," some would say. "An atrocity, a faux pas, a terrible blunder," others would claim. After all, this African man was a descendent of Ham and the object of a terrible and ancient curse that is far greater than history or the cross—or so some would claim. The truth is that God doesn't make mistakes, faux pas, or blunders like we do. The truth is that the people who invested their lives in promoting the so-called "curse of Ham" theory have wasted their breath on a curse gone astray.

> *He who pursues righteousness and loyalty finds life, righteousness and honor. A wise man scales the city of the mighty, and brings down the* **stronghold in which they trust** *(Proverbs 21:21-22).*

Righteousness is essentially "rightness or God's way of doing something." I should warn you that I'm going after a stronghold in this chapter. I want you to stay with me because there is a very strong possibility that this particular stronghold has affected your life for evil one way or another. Regardless of how it has affected us, the effect is always negative. I'm out to *demolish* this ungodly stronghold. I want to reduce it to dust under our feet in the name of Jesus, and the only way to do that is to pursue God's way of doing things.

### Strongholds, Arguments, and Pretensions

Paul put his spiritual finger on the problem behind this stronghold when he wrote, "[Our spiritual weapons]…have divine power to demolish strongholds. We demolish *arguments* and every *pretension* that sets itself up against the knowledge of God, and we take captive every thought to make it obedient to Christ" (2 Cor. 10:4-5 NIV).

I've heard it said that the first casualty in war is the truth. Have you ever heard someone say, "Ham was cursed; therefore, all black people are cursed"? One of the deepest divisions in the Church, especially in North America and South Africa, has been the racial barrier.[2] God wants to say something to us about His Word that is in stark contrast with the misguided opinions of some people concerning "the curse of Ham." God says, "It's a curse gone astray." Read this brief Scripture passage about the incident between Noah and Ham and consider what comes to your mind:

> Now the sons of Noah who came out of the ark were **Shem and Ham and Japheth; and Ham was the father of Canaan.** These three were the sons of Noah; and from these the whole earth was populated. Then Noah began farming and planted a vineyard. And he drank of the wine and became drunk, and uncovered himself inside his tent. And **Ham, the father of Canaan,** saw the nakedness of his father, and told his two brothers outside. But Shem and Japheth took a garment and laid it upon both their shoulders and walked backward and covered the nakedness of their father; and their faces were turned away, so that they did not see their father's nakedness. When Noah awoke from his wine, **he knew what his youngest son** had done to him. So he said, **"Cursed be Canaan;** a servant of servants he shall be to his brothers" (Genesis 9:18-25).

Pause right there and underline the word *youngest*. There is no Hebrew word for "youngest," nor is there a Hebrew word for "grandson." The language only differentiates between younger and greater. Context is the only way you can distinguish between "youngest" and "younger." To see *who* Noah was talking about, you have to look at his words before or after the phrase, "his youngest son." The Bible says, "When Noah awoke from his wine, he knew what *his youngest son* had done to him. So he said, 'Cursed be *Canaan*; a servant of servants he shall be to his brothers' " (Gen. 9:24-25). Now what "youngest son" did Noah curse? You may have to look at your Bible a second time because you are going to *read Canaan* and *think Ham*. Put your finger there and say, "Here is the problem."

## Who Did Noah Curse?

The stronghold I'm demolishing in this chapter is the "myth-turned-reality" called "the curse of Ham." In the very recent past (the last 400 years of human history), certain Church leaders used their offices of respect and leadership in their churches to wrongly justify the enslavement of African people by quoting Genesis 9:25. It is said that a respected preacher made this argument before the ruling legislative body of South Africa in a sermon in the 1940's, and his message helped advance the movement to establish *apartheid* (Afrikaans for "apart-hood"), a series of laws that made repressive racial discrimination against blacks and nonwhites a national policy. These arguments weren't limited to South Africa. Many preachers in North America have also used their pulpits to publicly justify the practice and promotion of slavery and racism on this continent for centuries—all based on the erroneous interpretation of this Scripture in Genesis 9.

This stronghold continues to enslave millions of people mentally, socially, and even spiritually in our day. Despite major advances in civil rights and Federal laws concerning equality of opportunity, many African-Americans and other "people of color" carry chains of slavery around with them in their hearts and thought patterns.

This isn't a whining complaint from an African-American author; it is a statement of fact from a minister of reconciliation who is determined to demolish this and every other stronghold afflicting God's people—regardless of their color, gender, or ethnic origin. This isn't a major plank in some social action agenda either; it is a passionate embrace of the biblical command, "Therefore, we are ambassadors for Christ, as though God were entreating through us; we beg you on behalf of Christ, be reconciled to God" (2 Cor. 5:20). The problem with the "curse of Ham," and in most cases like it, is that God's Word doesn't say what *people* say it says. Look for yourself and ask, "Who did God curse?"

"Well, God cursed Ham and that's why black folks were made slaves."

*He did? My Bible says it was **Noah** who did the cursing, not God.*

"Okay, Noah cursed Ham."

*He did? My Bible says Noah cursed **Canaan**, Ham's son.*

"Well, how about the verse that says, 'Noah knew what his son had done to him'? That's Ham. Case closed."

*Don't close the case yet. My Bible says Noah knew "what his **youngest son** had done to him" (Gen. 9:24). If you want to be a literalist, then **that would be Japheth**, not Ham. If you want to be accurate, then you would understand that "youngest son" is a Hebraic term in Jewish genealogy for son, grandson, or male descendents in general. Jesus was a son of David, and both Israel and Jacob are synonyms for the descendents of Abraham. It was the face of Canaan, **the youngest son of Ham**, that came to Noah's hungover mind as the culprit in the crime that produced a curse gone astray.*

I've presented the most common arguments in these few brief paragraphs, but we need to compare "the knowledge of God" to the claims used to support the stronghold of racial prejudice in America and South Africa. The same could be said of other strongholds of bondage such as gender bias ("let the women keep silent [and thus be of secondary importance] in the churches"); the "clergy/laity" division in which we have recreated the "priests as mediators" theology that Jesus came to do away with; and other biases against singles, divorced people, poor people, Roman Catholics, and sinners in general! Although God obviously loves sinners, many Christians seem to go out of their way to point them to hell rather than to Heaven.

## Amazing Fact: "Second Ain't Third"

*And Noah was five hundred years old, and Noah became the father of* **Shem, Ham, and Japheth** (Genesis 5:32).

*And Noah became the father of three sons:* **Shem, Ham, and Japheth** (Genesis 6:10).

*On the very same day* **Noah and Shem and Ham and Japheth,** *the sons of Noah, and Noah's wife and the three wives of his sons with them, entered the ark* (Genesis 7:13).

*Now the sons of Noah who came out of the ark were* **Shem and Ham and Japheth;** *and* **Ham was the father of Canaan** (Genesis 9:18).

*Now these are the records of the generations of* **Shem, Ham, and Japheth,** *the sons of Noah; and sons were born to them after the flood* (Genesis 10:1)

*And* **the sons of Ham** *were Cush and Mizraim and Put and Canaan* (Genesis 10:6).

*And the sons of Cush were Seba, Havilah, Sabta, Raama, and Sabteca; and the sons of Raamah were Sheba and Dedan. And Cush became the father of Nimrod; he began to be a mighty one in the earth* (1 Chronicles 1:9-10).

When the Bible lists the sons of Noah, who always ends up in the middle? Ham. Genealogies have always been important in the Jewish culture, but this was especially true in ancient times. God's Word gives careful attention to who is mentioned first, and who follows who in order where genealogies are concerned. The only exceptions occur when God is specifically adjusting genealogical listings to reflect a *different* spiritual ranking. This is the case when we say, "Abraham, Isaac, and Jacob." Isaac was not Abraham's oldest boy; Ishmael was, and Jacob was *not* Isaac's oldest son; Esau was.

The problem was that Esau sold his birthright to Jacob, so he lost out. Now once God makes that kind of change in the batting lineup, the new lineup permanently replaces the old from that day on. This doesn't happen with Ham. No matter how often the sons of Noah show up in Scripture, Ham always lands in the middle, like the ham in a ham sandwich. That is because God never changed the birth order of Noah's sons, and *that* is because neither God nor Noah cursed Ham. *Canaan* was the culprit who earned the curse of his grandfather. History bears this out.

## Was Ham Wrong to Tell?

Many people have carefully ignored Noah's extremely clear and carefully chosen words when he awoke "the morning after" and said, "Cursed be *Canaan*; a *servant of servants* he shall be to his brothers" (Gen. 9:25). They automatically stick in Ham's name in place of Canaan's, and then they back up to verse 22 where the Bible says Ham saw that his father was naked and said, "Ah ha!" Now Noah, whom the Bible calls a righteous man, drank some especially potent post-flood wine, got drunk, and lay uncovered inside his tent where Ham found him. Have you lived in a house with a lot of other people around? Once in a while you are going to see a family member in an embarrassing situation. About all you can say is, "Oops, I didn't know," and hurriedly walk out. If this has never happened to you, then you are the exception rather than the rule. Now if you found someone in Noah's state in a *tent*, where just anyone could barge in, you might say to somebody, "We need to get so-and-so covered up."

How would you respond? Ham came out and said to his brothers, "Dad's lying in the tent, and he doesn't have a stitch on." (The Hebrew term translated as "told" in this passage, nagad, is used 362 times in the Old Testament. It is the most commonly used word for "told, reported, described, announced, etc."3) Shem and Japheth promptly got a blanket and backed into the tent to cover up Noah's nakedness. I suggest to you that anyone who says Noah awakened and was angry at Ham is "reading into" the biblical record. To say that Ham disregarded his father's honor and blabbed about his dad's nakedness is pure fabrication.

Ask yourself why the Bible keeps alluding to the fact that Ham is "the father of Canaan." When Noah woke up, he knew that he *had been* uncovered (remember that his sons had covered him while he was still asleep). He also realized or remembered something that had happened to him, and many theologians today suggest that Canaan had attacked him homosexually (more on that later). No one but God *knows* if that is true or not, but I do know that whatever took place that night, history tells us it was Canaan and his descendents who were somehow affected by it. Whatever it was that Canaan did to Noah, it repulsed the patriarch enough to cause him to curse Canaan specifically. Remember that Noah awoke from his wine-induced sleep and realized or remembered what his *youngest son* had done to him, not what his *middle son* had done. As anyone can tell you, "second ain't third," even by liberal modern math standards.

## Look for a Crooked Man Walking Crooked Miles

There is an anonymous nursery rhyme entitled "There Was a Crooked Man" that goes like this:

There was a crooked man, and he went a crooked mile,
He found a crooked sixpence against a crooked stile;
He bought a crooked cat, which caught a crooked mouse,
And they all lived together in a little crooked house.

The Bible puts it this way, "So then, you will know them by their fruits" (Mt. 7:20). When you're looking for a man worthy of a curse who received a curse, then you should find evidence of the curse and the cause of the curse in his "house" or history. Ham's house is three-parts blessed and only one-part cursed. The Bible says, "And the sons of Ham were Cush and Mizraim and Put and Canaan" (Gen. 10:6). Ham's three oldest sons seemed to prosper throughout much of their history. The most famous descendent from these three sons was Nimrod, the son of Cush. Whether he was ultimately a good guy or a bad guy, we can only guess. But the Bible commentary about Nimrod doesn't seem to have any hint of a curse in it: "And Cush became the father of Nimrod; he began to be a mighty one in the earth" (1 Chron. 1:10). Another verse says:

> *Now Cush became the father of Nimrod; he became a mighty one on the earth. He was a mighty hunter before the Lord; therefore it is said, "Like Nimrod a mighty hunter before the Lord." And the beginning of his kingdom was Babel and Erech and Accad and Calneh, in the land of Shinar. From that land he went forth into Assyria, and built Nineveh and Rehoboth-Ir and Calah, and Resen between Nineveh and Calah; that is the great city* (Genesis 10:8-12).

When the Bible says Nimrod was a mighty hunter "before the Lord," it uses the same language that is translated in many other places as "in the presence of the Lord." However, my Bible does *not* say Nimrod was a mighty rebel before the Lord. The cities that Nimrod built were later known for less-than-godly deeds, such as the erection of the Tower of Babel, but then again the sin at Babel involved men of every line and lineage. It is there that God split humanity apart into nations with distinct languages. No specific curse is mentioned there, just the usual "fallen man" kind of activity. The great city of Ninevah mattered so much to God that He sent Jonah there to preach judgment, and God spared the city after the people repented. There is no sign of a curse there. The "crooked man" is missing from this picture.

Ham's second son, Mizraim, was the ancestor of the Egyptians and other tribes in close proximity to them. In chapter 15 of the Book of Genesis, God spoke to Abram in a deep sleep and told him that his descendents (as yet unborn) would be strangers in a country not their own where they would be enslaved and mistreated for 400 years (see Gen. 15:12-14). The "enslavers" here are the Egyptians, descendents of *Ham's* son, Mizraim. There's no hint of a curse here, although God said He would punish Egypt for mistreating Israel. In the end, Egypt is blessed by God: "Whom the Lord of hosts has blessed, saying, 'Blessed is Egypt My people, and Assyria the work of My hands, and Israel My inheritance'" (Is. 19:25)!

Ham's third son, Phut or Put, was the ancestor of the modern Persian people. These people didn't follow after God, but neither did they have a specific curse on their heads that was experienced any more or less than by anyone else who failed to follow God. Canaan, however, is another story. Here we find a crooked man with an entire atlas of "crooked miles" to his credit.

## Canaan's Long Crooked Mile

According to Genesis 10:15-18, Canaan was the father of Sidon, his firstborn, and of Heth, the Jebusites, the Amorites, the Girgashites, the Hivites, the Arkites, the Sinites, the Arvadites, the Zemarites, and the Hamathites. The Canaanites occupied territory that ranged from Sidon to Gera as far as Gaza, and then beyond the cities of Sodom and Gomorrah. Many years later, David and his men would have to dislodge the "Jebusites" from Jebus, on the site where Jerusalem sits today (see 2 Sam. 5:6-7).

God told Abram in a vision that his descendents would return "in the fourth generation" because *the sin of the Amorites* had not yet reached its full measure (see Gen. 15:16). Then God cut a supernatural covenant with Abram, giving him the land occupied by the same *Canaanite* people mentioned in Genesis 10:15-18. He mentioned by name the Kenites, Hittites, Perizzites, Amorites, the Canaanites, Girgashites, and the Jebusites (see Gen. 15:19-21). Later on,

God ordered the Israelites to "utterly destroy" these tribes because of their total religious and sexual depravity. These tribes practiced ritual sacrifice of children and adults to demonic entities, and were noted for incredible sexual perversion involving children, adults, and animals. It was during Israel's conquest of the Promised Land that the ultimate curse on Canaan's descendents came to pass (for example, see Joshua 9:27–10:40).

## The Sodom and Gomorrah Connection

What is the "sin of the Amorites" that God mentioned in Genesis 15:16? We get a strong clue in Genesis chapter 18 where God reveals to Abraham that He intends to destroy Sodom and Gomorrah. Abraham immediately went into the intercessory mode because his nephew, Lot, lived in Sodom along with his wife and family. He asked God to spare the city if He found 50 righteous people in the cities, and God agreed. Then, step by step, Abraham kept reducing the minimum number until he finally stopped at ten righteous people (see Gen. 18:22-33).

If we have any doubt about why God wanted to destroy these two cities, it should be cleared up by the Bible's description of how the residents treated two angels sent to investigate the cities. Now the truth is that the Lord didn't find ten righteous people in those cities; He found one—Lot. When God sent two angels to Sodom that evening, they found Lot sitting in the gate of the city. He got up to meet them and bowed down with his face to the ground. He urged them to spend the night in his house but when they said they would just spend the night in the square, Lot insisted so strongly that they finally went to his house and God's statements were quickly confirmed:

*Before they lay down, the men of the city, the men of Sodom, surrounded the house, both young and old, all the people from every quarter; and they called to Lot and said to him,*

*"Where are the men who came to you tonight? Bring them out to us that we may have [sexual] relations with them"* (Genesis 19:4-5).

This problem wasn't limited to a small minority of men—the Bible says, "...the men of Sodom surrounded the house, both young and old, *all the people* from every quarter" converged on Lot's house! The problem with the men and boys of Sodom and Gomorrah is clearly described by the English word *homosexuality*. It was homosexuality in its most blatant and virulent form. This Canaanite city was infected with an all-out plague of deviant sexual behavior. With this same "sin of the Amorites" showing up throughout Canaan's line, isn't it logical, probable, and plain common sense to believe that Canaan might have had a sexual deviancy problem to one extent or another? It sure makes you want to look at the so-called "curse of Ham" situation in a new light. The people whom God "gave over" to the Israelites when they possessed the Promised Land were of the heritage and seed of Canaan. This alone should be enough to conclusively confirm that Ham wasn't cursed—Canaan was.

A few of the Canaanites managed to avoid extermination at Joshua's hands, which set up another opportunity for Noah's curse on Canaan and his descendents to come to pass:

*Now this is the account of the **forced labor** [slavery] which King Solomon levied to build the house of the Lord, his own house, the Millo, the wall of Jerusalem, Hazor, Megiddo, and Gezer. ... As for all the people who were left of the **Amorites**, the **Hittites**, the **Perizzites**, the **Hivites** and the **Jebusites**, who were not of the sons of Israel, their descendants who were left after them in the land whom the sons of Israel were unable to destroy utterly, **from them Solomon levied forced laborers**, even to this day* (1 Kings 9:15,20-21).

While the descendents of Canaan were falling deeper into deviant sexual and religious practices, being destroyed by the Israelites (who were descendents of Shem) and enslaved by Solomon, the other Hamatic descendents from his other three sons were prospering. The Psalmist recorded under inspiration that God called Egypt the "land of Ham" (see Ps. 105:23,27), and the long-term success of the Egyptian dynasties is well established in history. They were educated, highly advanced in mathematics, and dominated the world at different times.

Ham's folk weren't ignorant. Modern scientists are still trying to figure out things that the Egyptians had mastered thousands of years ago. Our best scientists and engineers still haven't figured out how they managed to move all those monolithic stones around the desert to build the pyramids and other massive buildings. Our best medical minds don't know how the Egyptians preserved the mummies so well either—it is a science that is lost.

Assyria and Ninevah were also Hamitic lands, and it doesn't take a deep study of the Bible to realize that they were not in slavery to anyone. The "hanging gardens of Babylon" are listed as one of the seven wonders of the ancient world, and the Babylonian and Assyrian empires were renowned for their power and domination in their heydays. This isn't slavery; this is growth. Even those Hamitic descendents in what theologians used to call "the darkest part of Africa" were busy building incredible empires, writing languages, and producing cultures that spanned hundreds of years. They were world famous for their wealth in gold and jewels. That is why the Bible goes into such detail when describing such Hamatic Bible characters as the Queen of Sheba (see 1 Kings 10:1-10) and the Ethiopian eunuch who was the *treasurer* for "Candace, queen of the Ethiopians" (see Acts 8:27). No curse is in sight with these descendents of Ham!

You cannot take 400 years of recent activity in 10,000 years of human civilization and say, "Well, the last 400 years of slavery for black folks is the fulfillment of prophecy of Noah over Ham." For thousands of years, Ham's descendents were no one's slaves. They were building cities and creating their own languages and world-dominating civilizations. In Jesus' day, there were probably more so-called "barbarian" slaves (from warlike Germanic tribes) in the Middle East than there were non-white slaves. Does this mean that they were cursed by God too? No! In the days of Jesus and Paul, slavery was a legitimate practice. *Anyone could end up as a slave in those days, regardless of their race, creed, color, or national origin.*

If you got caught at the wrong party, you could be made a slave. If you failed to pay your bills or owed a debt you couldn't pay, you or your entire family could be made slaves. If you were on the wrong crew ship, you could be made a slave. If you were a free man with a lot of money in your home country, but were captured by pirates at sea or by robbers on a trade route, you could become a slave for the rest of your life. Even princes became slaves at times.

### What if Ham Really Was Cursed?

All right, I'll answer that just in case you really want to be unreasonable. What if every black person (including me) is under a curse because we are descendents of Ham? I'll let God answer that one: "Christ redeemed us from the curse of the Law, having *become a curse for us...*" (Gal. 3:13). No matter what curse is out there floating around, any breathing human being can "duck it" *by going straight to the cross.* (Now there really was no "if" to this question, but this answer should help anyone who still has lingering fears and doubts planted there by society or people who still like to curse Ham.)

A young man came up to me and said, "I had a discussion with a guy in my church who said, 'Aren't blacks cursed?' " This man had doubts because African-Americans have heard the myth for so long that they involuntarily agree with it half the time. "Well, can 10,000 theologians be wrong?" Shoot, yeah. No, *heck yeah!* The thing I love the most about Jesus is that if you can find your way into His family, then you are acceptable. All you have to do is pick up the Book and turn to Matthew chapter 1 to see what the Bible calls "the genealogy of Jesus Christ." There you will find four outstanding (and absolutely controversial) women in the Lord's genealogy.

*Tamar* was the daughter-in-law of Judah who tricked him into having incestuous sexual relations with her after he refused to honor the law of Israel. She demanded that he allow her to marry his youngest son when her own husband(s) died without fathering children, and he had refused. Judah thought he was having relations with an unknown prostitute at the time, and when he found out that his daughter-in-law was pregnant, he wanted to kill her as an adulteress. When Tamar produced proof that *he* was the father, Judah had to confess his own sin and acknowledge her two sons as his own (see Gen. 38:6-30)! Her sons, Perez and Zerah, are prominently mentioned as earthly ancestors of Jesus Christ (see Mt. 1:3).

Rahab, *a Canaanite prostitute,* shows up in both Matthew chapter 1 and the Book of Judges. If men had anything to do with it, she would have struck out on two counts—she was a citizen of Jericho, a Canaanite city and so under "the curse," and she was a prostitute. We're not talking about prime "Messiah" material here—or are we? God seems to think so (see Mt. 1:5; Josh. 6:25).

Then there's Ruth the *Moabitess.* The Bible says, "No Ammonite or Moabite shall enter the assembly of the Lord; none of their descendants, even to the tenth generation, shall ever enter the assembly of the Lord" (Deut. 23:3). Ten generations is a long time to wait to be saved or "accepted" by a family. Somehow, by the grace and preordained plan of God, Ruth got into the family of God. She became the great grandmother of King David, and speaking "evangelastically," she became the great, great, great grandmother of Jesus Christ (see Mt. 1:5-16). I won't even go into the story of Bathsheba and how she landed in Jesus' family tree. Aren't you glad that those curses don't affect you either?

One of the first questions that comes up in any conversation about the reconciliation of races is this: "Well, what if my son wants to marry somebody who is not of our race?" My answer is simple and well thought-out: "Is she of the *human* race? Now if she isn't, then I can understand your concern." I remember the time a man asked my brother, John, "Do you believe in mixed marriages?" He instantly replied, "No, I don't think that Christians ought to marry non-Christians." When the Bible says "be not unequally yoked" to one another (see 2 Cor. 6:14 KJV), the Lord isn't talking about racial mixtures or cultural blending problems. The only issue God cares about is the Christ issue. That is all that matters in His Kingdom. Beyond that, He doesn't care if you are Jewish, Gentile, bond or free, male or female, or rich or poor. Dr. Mark Chironna says that there are only two races on the earth: "One is racing towards Heaven; the other is racing toward hell. Which race are you in? One is a marathon and the other is a sprint."

The stronghold of racism isn't a human problem; it is a human symptom of a *spiritual* problem. We need to tear down the stronghold that has successfully invaded and wrecked human lives and divided the Church for centuries. All of us who call upon the name of Jesus, regardless of our color, nationality, or gender, need to declare and claim our freedom in Christ so we can offer it to others without shame or apology.

### Endnotes

1. *PC Bible Atlas*, Coppyright 1993, Parsons Technology.

2. I must add that my wife and I discovered that many churches in South Africa had chosen to ignore or dismiss

the apartheid policy. These truly multicultural churches were the true pioneers behind the downfall of apartheid and the unity of the brethren under the banner of Jesus. In this sense, the South African Church as a whole is much more advanced in the area of reconciliation than many churches in America!

3. James Strong, *Strong's Exhaustive Concordance of the Bible* (Peabody, Massachusetts: Hendrickson Publishers, n.d.), *told*, (5046).

# Chapter 12

# Now That I've Found My Roots, What Should I Do With Them?

I have a wonderful friend (who happens to be Caucasian), who kept telling me about another friend of his. He said, "Garlington, you need to meet this guy." For two months he kept encouraging me to meet this guy, and he finally arranged for both of us to meet at a party at his house. When he introduced us, I was shocked. I told the man, "I didn't know *you* were black," and he said, "I didn't know you were black either." Then it dawned on both of us that our mutual friend had never discussed skin color or race with either one of us. All he talked about was his friendship with both of us.

This was a bittersweet revelation. On the one hand, I wish we would all see one another as that mutual friend saw us—as people of worth and value. But I was saddened to discover the hidden stereotype in my mind that thought, *This other friend sounds so neat that he couldn't be talking about a black guy*. Now that is called self-hatred. We tend to create our own details when people fail to describe a person's gender, racial or ethnic background, and economic status. Those stereotypical details that you come up with can reveal a lot about *you.*

Somehow we need to learn how to listen to people talk about Christians whom we haven't met without having to ask, "What church do they belong to?" We need to see them God's way, without regard to whether they are male or female, Jew or Gentile, bond or free, circumcised or uncircumcised, or sprinkled or dunked. I'm tired of telling someone, "I have a great friend, a preacher..." only to be interrupted in police interrogation style: "How was he baptized? Does he use wine or grape juice in the communion?" If I say, "Those are religious decisions," they say, "Yes, pastor, but very important around here." *It has been amazing to me to see how people who don't know a whole lot about theology can get along so well with God—until theologians come along and break up the fellowship.*

Author and counselor Leanne Payne wrote about a white pastor named David who was battling severe suicidal urges. (I mention his race only because it is important to his case.) She described this pastor's story in her landmark book, *Crisis in Masculinity.*[1] David was one of five children, two of whom had already committed suicide in their 30's, and another had attempted suicide but failed. Now David himself was sinking into deeper despair and the author was trying to find the root of his pain and bring healing to him through Christ. He grew up in poverty in the southern sharecropper tradition in Georgia, and his father was harshly authoritarian toward his wife and children.

In her book, Payne emphasized that sin is not wiped out by time, but only through repentance and the blood of Jesus. She discovered that Pastor David's problem began two generations before his birth through a family trauma that had to be uncovered, dealt with, and the sin confessed before he could receive physiological and spiritual healing.

This principle may well apply to many who read this book, and it is at the heart of biblical reconciliation.

## The Man Who Never Was

At some point, David's father asked a family member to take him to the family cemetery in an out-of-the-way location in North Carolina. Once he got there, he began to search an overgrown hill in the cemetery. Just as he found the grave he was looking for, another "old timer" showed up who recognized David's father. He looked at the grave and suddenly began to reminisce on its history—totally ignoring the frantic efforts of David's father to stop him. He said, "I remember when the old Indian, your father, was refused burial in the Christian burial ground. I still remember when they brought him up here to rest."[2]

The problem was that the grave was the resting place of a grandfather whose name and very existence had never once been acknowledged to David or the other four grandchildren. It was a testimony of racial prejudice, ignorance, and hatred of an isolated community that stretched back to colonial times. The grandfather's American Indian heritage had disqualified him for a "decent Christian burial," and this seemingly white family had totally erased his existence in shame. Pastor David and his surviving siblings were still wrestling with this almost three-quarters of a century later!

Leanne Payne writes, "As a child *sees itself* through the eyes of others, so this family saw and accepted itself according to the community's verdict and estimate....In their attempts to accept themselves and to find acceptance in the very community that rejected their progenitor, they had ended by attempting to wipe the man's very existence from memory. There is no greater rejection than this: the failure to recognize that a person *is*, or has *ever been*."[3]

Pastor David finally received the peace of God when Leanne Payne prayed that God would bless the Indian in

Pastor David. She said, "…it was as if he integrated with a long lost part of himself. Multitudes of black people in the United States, and especially black men, need the very type of illumination prayer, and healing that Pastor David received. The crisis in masculinity among blacks in our country can and must be healed. May it be so, and soon. Needless to say, Indians, blacks, and Jews, and others who have experienced great rejection due to race have special needs in the area of healing of memories."[4]

Years ago when I read that, I said, "God, if ever there is a spiritual answer to the spiritual problem dividing us, *this is it*." If I keep telling you that I hate you because of your skin, because of your limitations, because of your sex, or because of your ethnic background, then at some point you will begin to hate yourself. And your rejection of yourself will be even greater than my rejection of you. What chance of recovery do you have if I take something as authoritative as the Word of God and twist it to undergird and justify my rejection of you? Who can fight against God? We know that God doesn't support or say these kinds of things, but a lie that is *perceived* as truth still has the power to destroy us indiviually as well as a society.

This is our challenge: We must pull down the stronghold in which the mighty have trusted, whether we are Caucasian, African-American, Asian-American, American Indian, or Polynesian. We need to pull down the strongholds of prejudice and division wherever we find them, and lift up Jesus Christ in their place!

From the beginning of this book, I've asked the question, "What do we do with the ministry of reconciliation?" I'm looking for the *right* answer, although I realize that you might be as confused as the students in the Sunday school class who have come to believe that the "safe" answer to the teacher's question is always "Jesus." When their teacher asked, "Children, who killed Goliath?" Annie said, "Jesus."

The teacher said, "No, it was really David. Now Jesus helped him, but it was David." Then she said, "All right, kids, who led the children of Israel through the Red Sea?" Excitement filled the room and hands filled the air as the boys and girls cried, "O-h-h, choose me, teacher. Choose me!" She pointed to one boy and said, "Okay, Sammy, who did it?" He answered with supreme confidence, "Jesus!" The teacher said, "No, it's really Moses." She looked around and pointed to a boy named Bobby and said, "All right, one more question. Bobby, what's gray and furry, has a bushy tail, breaks nuts with his teeth, and runs up and down a tree?" Bobby was trapped, but he said, "Teacher, I know the answer is Jesus, but it sure sounds like a squirrel."

### Knowledge and the Jailhouse Blues

The moral to this somewhat confusing story is, "No matter what answer you think it is, go with the one that is in the Bible." Now I'm looking for a right answer. "What do we do with the ministry of reconciliation?" The right answer is: "In a divided society, the Church must model unity." Doesn't the Bible say that the truth will set you free? *It does not.* It says, "...You *shall know* the truth, and the truth shall make you free" (Jn. 8:32). You can sit in a jail cell and have the keys sitting next to you that will unlock the door. But if you have never seen a key before, then you are going to continue sitting in that jail.

"How long have you been in here?" you ask.

"I've been in here about five years," I say.

"Why don't you use the key?" you ask.

"What key? What is a key?"

"Those things right there—those symbols lying on the bed beside you."

"You mean I can get out of here with these?" I ask.

"Yeah, any one of them will get you out," you say.

So when I open the door, I would almost certainly tell you, "Man, if I'd known this, I'd have been out a long time ago." The Church has been asleep in a jail of her own making while the keys of the Kingdom and of reconciliation have been within our reach the whole time! Paul describes part of it in his Epistle to the Philippians:

*For we are the true circumcision, who worship in the Spirit of God and **glory in Christ Jesus** and **put no confidence in the flesh*** (Philippians 3:3).

We have problems getting along and living the Christ-like life because we put our confidence in the *flesh* and glory in our human heritage. Paul had a lot to boast about if you look at his human heritage and accomplishments as a rabbi, Pharisee, Roman citizen, and heir-apparent to Gamaliel, one of the greatest Jewish teachers. But Paul had a life-changing encounter with Jesus Christ, and all he had to say about his considerable earthly credentials was, "...I count all things to be loss in view of the surpassing value of knowing Christ Jesus my Lord, for whom I have suffered the loss of all things, and count them but *rubbish* in order that I may gain Christ" (Phil. 3:8).

Paul completes the answer in his letters to the Colossians and to the Ephesian believers:

*As you therefore have received Christ Jesus the Lord, so walk in Him, having been firmly rooted and now being built up in Him and established in your faith, just as you were instructed, and overflowing with gratitude* (Colossians 2:6-7).

*For this reason, I bow my knees before the Father, from whom every family in heaven and on earth derives its name, that He would grant you, according to the riches of His glory, to be strengthened with power through His Spirit in the inner man; so that Christ may dwell in your hearts through faith; and that you, being rooted and grounded in love* (Ephesians 3:14-17).

Paul told us to be *rooted and built up in Jesus*. Then he also said we are to be *rooted and established or grounded in love*. We should appreciate "being rooted" in God and His Kingdom. I remember when Alex Haley's best-selling book, *Roots*, was released, and later made into a movie. All of a sudden people began to think about their background—people of every conceivable ethnic and racial background. Their genealogy suddenly became important to them as they sensed their need for relatedness, not just in the present, but in the past. Many of us put a greater emphasis on our roots then we ought to, but is important to know your roots.

### "It Do Make a Difference"

I heard a story some time ago about a pastor in the South who had a radio broadcast. He was well-liked, but he wasn't noted for his theological ability. One day he received a call from a listener who said, "Dear Pastor, I was reading about the eight sons that Milcah bare. What can you tell me about them?" (see Gen. 22:23) The elderly minister paused for a moment and said, "Well, I want to be careful before I give you an answer. Now the first thing that I want to say is: 'Them weren't no ordinary sons, them eight sons.' And the second thing that I want to say is: 'That weren't no ordinary bear.' And the last thing that I want to say is, 'It do make a difference who your pappy is.' "

"It do make a difference who your pappy is." It is important to know where you come from and with whom. But it is even more important to understand that God's view of "family" is a lot different from our view of family. When God thinks of family, He thinks of a family that exists in Heaven and on earth. That means that in His all-wise eyes, we are all part of *one family*.

### Dirty Greek and Three Concepts

I want to share three concepts with you to seal our discussion of reconciliation. The first one is *one source*, the second is *one flesh*, and the third is *one finish*. Then I'm going to teach you a bad word in Greek and a couple of other things and we'll be done.

God is sovereign. He is in control. That means that when God tells us about our roots, He is right—no matter what history teachers, anthropologists, and sociologists tell us. God knows more about your roots—and about the anthropologist's roots—than anyone else on the planet. When we go to Him in prayer and trust His Word, life becomes clear. Issues become clear when you remember that *God is right* whenever He speaks, even when we don't understand. (And we thought that privilege was reserved exclusively for evolutionists!)

Do you remember the verse we quoted in the very first chapter? "But the *Jerusalem above* is free; she is *our mother*" (Gal. 4:26). We have the same mother in Christ. Now look at this Scripture passage recording Paul's words to the Epicurean and Stoic philosophers who met with him at the Areopagus in Athens, Greece:

> *The God who made the world and all things in it, since He is Lord of heaven and earth, does not dwell in temples made with hands; neither is He served by human hands, as though He needed anything, since He Himself gives to all life and breath and all things; and **He made from one, every nation of mankind** to live on all the face of the earth, having **determined their appointed times**, and **the boundaries of their habitation**, that they should seek God, if perhaps they might grope for Him and find Him, though He is not far from each one of us; for in Him we live and move and exist, as even some of your own poets have said, "For we also are His offspring"* (Acts 17:24-28).

The King James Version says God "hath made *of one blood* all nations of men for to dwell on all the face of the earth" (Acts 17:26b). God determined the moment of your birth all by Himself—He didn't need or ask for anyone else's opinion on it. He also determined exactly *where* you would land in this earth. In my case, He said, "Garlington, you're going to Buffalo, New York. Not only are you going to Buffalo, but I'm also putting you in the public housing projects in Buffalo." Dear Jesus.

### No Orphans in God's Kingdom

According to Psalm 68, God also decides what family setting we grow up in. The psalmist wrote, "A father of the fatherless and a judge for the widows, is God in His holy habitation. God makes a home for the lonely [in families]…" (Ps. 68:5-6). The third thing He does is determine who will be in your family. Now don't get mad, because even though God is sovereign, *everything that He does is redemptive in its ultimate purpose.* He's not sitting up in Heaven saying, "I wonder how I can make them more miserable today than yesterday?" He is a good God, and He places us in families. There is no such thing as a Lone Ranger in God's family. Even the Lone Ranger had Tonto (or at least until the Indians came after him).

> But **God gives it a body just as He wished**, *and to each of the seeds a body of its own. All flesh is not the same flesh, but* **there is one flesh of men**, *and another flesh of beasts, and another flesh of birds, and another of fish. There are also heavenly bodies and earthly bodies, but the glory of the heavenly is one, and the glory of the earthly is another* (1 Corinthians 15:38-40).

Everything that God does is ultimately *redemptive* in purpose. God determines our bodies, so if He made you a woman, then it gives Him delight for you to be one. Whether He made you tall or short, He's thrilled about it. Whoever and whatever you are, just put your hand up and say, "God, if You determined what I am, then I'm going to thank You for it all. I don't understand everything about it, but I welcome Your choice."

God says there is only one kind of human flesh. We look at flesh and we say, "Oh, there is some red flesh, and there is some brown flesh, and there is some pink flesh, right? And there is some olive-colored flesh, there is some light brown flesh, and there is some dark brown flesh, and there is some really dark brown flesh." Yes, there are all kinds of *colors* of flesh, but only one *kind* of human flesh. What does God see? *One flesh.* If you were able to somehow peel back the part of the body that has pigment in the skin, you would find that your flesh looks the same as my flesh—regardless of our racial, ethnic, or cultural differences. That doesn't leave us much to crow about.

> *Thus says the Lord, "Let not a wise man boast of his wisdom, and let not the mighty man boast of his might, let not a rich man boast of his riches; but let him who boasts boast of this, that he understands and knows Me, that I am the Lord who exercises lovingkindness, justice, and righteousness on earth; for I delight in these things," declares the Lord* (Jeremiah 9:23-24).

There was a young Jewish boy who was born in Germany in 1879, who loved to play violin but who was generally considered "slow" because he had poor hand-to-eye coordination. He had difficulty in school where mindless drilling was the order of the day, but he loved to study abstract subjects like geometry and popular science at home. He failed his first college entrance exam for a university in Switzerland in 1895, and he enrolled in a secondary preparatory school and graduated in 1900 as a teacher of mathematics and physics. No school seemed to want him, and no one seemed to hold any great hopes for Albert Einstein, but he made it anyway. He wrote some of the fundamental papers that revolutionized the world of physics while working a mindless day job at the Swiss patent office in Bern as a technical "expert third class." Over the next 53 years, Einstein revolutionized scientific thought about matter and energy with his "General Theory of Relativity." Not bad for someone who was "slow."

## I Live in a Grass Hut

We are too quick to boast in the wrong things, and to put down other people for the worst of reasons. No matter how significant or special we think our pedigree is, it is irrelevant to God. His Word says, "For, 'ALL FLESH IS LIKE GRASS AND ALL ITS GLORY LIKE THE FLOWER OF GRASS. THE GRASS WITHERS, AND THE FLOWER FALLS OFF, BUT THE WORD OF THE LORD ABIDES FOREVER...' " (1 Pet. 1:24-25). God is saying that, basically, you and I live in "grass huts," and our huts (our bodies) are strictly temporary shelters built for short-term use. The Bible also helps bring perspective to our "credentials" for ministry and leadership when it says:

> *But God has chosen **the foolish things** of the world to shame the wise, and God has chosen **the weak things** of the world to shame the things which are strong, and **the base things** of the world and **the despised**, God has chosen, **the things that are not**, that He might nullify the things that are, **that no man should boast before God** (1 Corinthians 1:27-29).*

The mighty King Herod decided to deliver a great speech to his appreciative subjects in Caesarea, not realizing that they were only appeasing him so he would keep sending them food. He put on his best royal robes and made his royal speech in his best king-like manner. To his surprise and pleasure, the people kept shouting out, "The voice of a god and not of a man!" (Acts 12:22) The Bible says, "And immediately an angel of the Lord struck him because he did not give God the glory, and he was eaten by worms and died" (Acts 12:23).

No flesh glories in God's presence. "I am a 'daughter of the American Revolution.' " That's flesh, and you can't glory in His presence. "I can trace my lineage to George Washington."

That's flesh; you can't glory in His presence either. "I am a royal heir in direct line from the King of the Zulu nation." That is also flesh, so you can't glory in His presence. No matter how far you trace your "roots," your flesh will become either an idol or an obstacle separating you from your true heritage in Christ. That is why God's Word tells us this:

> *Therefore from now on we recognize no man according to the flesh; even though we have known Christ according to the flesh, yet now we know Him thus no longer. Therefore if any man is in Christ, he is a new creature; the old things passed away; behold, new things have come. Now all these things are from God, who reconciled us to Himself through Christ, and gave us the ministry of reconciliation* (2 Corinthians 5:16-18).

We are too preoccupied with flesh. The problem is on the inside. The truth is that corruption is always working in our flesh, and it started the moment you were conceived in your mother's womb, and it will not be interrupted until Jesus comes and changes you in His presence and in the midst of His coming. If He doesn't come before your body goes back to the dust from which it came, then you will await your new body in a better place. Did you ever pull dust particles apart and say, "I wonder if this was Chinese dust, Polish dust, or Ukrainian dust?" "Oh, this is dark dust—it must be Nigerian dust." No, that's not how it works. Dust is dust. We are all one flesh, and in Christ we all have the same mother.

### I Found My Roots...Now What?

The amazing thing in all this discussion of our weaknesses, flesh, and heritage as a fallen race is that *God is not ashamed of us.* We have one Source, and we come from one flesh. Now that you have found your roots, what do you do with them? We find an answer in Matthew's Gospel. "He who has found his life shall lose it, and he who has lost his life for My sake shall find it" (Mt. 10:39). Now that you know who you are, whether you are Korean, African, German, Ukrainian, Apache, Yugoslavian, or any of the various mixtures known as "Dutch Stew" or "Hawaiian Chop Suey," I have three things to say to you about our *one finish.* In other words, this is what you do with your "roots."

First of all, *lose it.* Second, *refuse* [*reff-use*] it because it is refuse and garbage. Third, *transfuse it.* Jesus gave us a perfect picture of how we should lose our roots and fleshly qualifications when He washed His disciples' feet:

> *Jesus, knowing that the Father had given all things into His hands, and that He had come forth from God, and was going back to God, rose from supper, and laid aside His garments; and taking a towel, He girded Himself about. Then He poured water into the basin, and began to wash the disciples' feet, and to wipe them with the towel with which He was girded* (John 13:3-5).

The Greek text here is often translated this way: "Jesus, knowing that He had come from God and was going back to God, got up, He took off His outer garment, and He served." You can't give away what you don't have, and you can't lay down something that you don't have to lay down. *I'm saying that it is really important for you to find out who you are,* but only because that is the only way *you can lay it down!* The first step in our God-ordained *one finish* is to lose our roots. That goes for each of us, and for every root we have, whether it's good or bad.

I promised to teach you a dirty Greek word, so here it is: *skubalon.*[5] That's the dirty Greek word Paul used to describe his genealogical roots, his academic achievements, and his high religious rank in the Jewish elite of his day. He put it this way: "More than that, I count all things to be loss in view of the surpassing value of knowing Christ Jesus my Lord, for whom I have suffered the loss of all things, and count

them but rubbish [*skubalon*] in order that I may gain Christ"
(Phil. 3:8).

**Ditch Your Doo-Doo Certificates**

Paul called his impeccable bloodline and biblical training
at the feet of Gamaliel refuse, garbage, trash, dung, and doo-
doo, the kind of stuff that is barely fit to throw out to your
dog. How could he do that? He simply compared it to the
roots that Jesus gave him on the road to Damascus. We all
need to say that about our roots too, whether they are precious and wonderful or hideous and destructive. It's all under the blood, and we belong to a new family now. Like it or
not, your roots in God's eyes are *skubalon*. They're dog doo-
doo compared to your roots in Christ. Ditch your "doo-doo
certificates" and receive your royal inheritance in Christ Jesus. The next step allows us to both *"reff-use"* and *transfuse*
our fleshly roots. (Get ready to shout.)

> *Immediately I was in the Spirit; and behold, a throne was
> standing in heaven, and One sitting on the throne. And He
> who was sitting was like a jasper stone and a sardius in ap-
> pearance; and there was a rainbow around the throne, like
> an emerald in appearance. ... And when the living crea-
> tures give glory and honor and thanks to Him who sits on
> the throne, to Him who lives forever and ever, the twenty-
> four elders will fall down before Him who sits on the throne,
> and will worship Him who lives forever and ever, and will
> **cast their crowns before the throne**, saying, "Worthy art
> Thou, our Lord and our God, to receive glory and honor
> and power; for Thou didst create all things, and because of
> Thy will they existed, and were created"* (Revelation 4:2-
> 3,9-11).

Are you crowned with glory and honor? (See Hebrews
2:9-10.) Do you have a crown for having run the race? (See
First Corinthians 9:24 and Hebrews 12:1.) Perhaps you *are*
somebody special in the earth or in the church because of

who your father and mother were. You may be able to re-hearse your genealogy all the way back to the American Revolution, or back to Africa or Ham. You may believe that you are a surviving relative of the last Russian Czar or a cousin twice removed of Queen Elizabeth. It doesn't really matter, because once you figure out what kind of crown you've got, you will just take it off and cast it at His feet when you come into His presence. Why? Because *no flesh* can glory in His presence. Take it off and cast it at His feet. Lose it, "reff-use" it, transfuse it. Allow Him to bring you close to Him and listen to Him say:

> *You are no longer part of the first Adam; you are now part of the second Adam. You are no longer natural; you are spiritual. You are no longer earthly, but you are heavenly. You are no longer like the earthly; you are like the heavenly. You are no longer corruptible; you are incorruptible. You are no longer perishable, but you are imperishable. You are no longer mortal; you are immortal. You no longer have an earthly citizenship, but you have a heavenly citizenship. You are not part of Jerusalem beneath; you are part of Jerusalem above. Sarah is your mother, not Hagar. You are no longer in bondage; you're in freedom. You are no longer literally circumcised; you are spiritually circumcised. You are no longer externally a Jew; you are internally a Jew. You are a new nation, you are a royal priesthood, you are the brand-new race that is showing forth the promises of God. If any person be in Christ, he or she is a new creature. All things are passed away; behold, all things have become new.*

### Remember to Take Out the Trash

If you feel it is necessary, then get some kind of intellectual appreciation for who you are. But once you find out who you are and where you came from, and once you have neatly packaged your genealogy and put your roots in right order, write this dirty Greek word all over it: *Skubalon!*

Dung! and lay it down beside Paul's garbage sack. It's time for us to spend our time with somebody who says, "I like you just the way you are—with your teeth in or with your teeth out." Only the Spirit of Christ can give us friends and co-workers like that!

God made you the way you are because it pleased Him to do so. Now the rest of us have to look at you with the same pleasure and unconditional acceptance! In the same way, you need to understand that God made me the way I am because it pleases Him. (And He didn't ask my opinion about it either, because I might have asked Him to make me a little taller.) Now you need to look at me with the same pleasure and unconditional acceptance!

Many years ago, a wonderful movie was released called, *The Chariots of Fire.* The central character was an outstanding Christian runner named Eric Liddell from Scotland who was asked to compete in the Olympics for Great Britain, but who refused to compromise his convictions by competing on Sunday, which he regarded as a day set apart unto God. Early in the film, someone asks this young man, "What is it about running that you like so much?" This is what he said (at least as well as I can remember it):

> "I believe God made me for a purpose,
> but He also made me fast.
> And when I run, I feel His pleasure."

When you are doing what God wants you to do, *you can feel His pleasure.* God is alive and well, and He is excited about what is going on in the earth today! If every now and then you put a hand up toward the Lord in Heaven and you feel like you have plugged into a 5,000-volt power line, then you've touched God. And if you go through your whole Christian experience and have never felt the electrifying touch of God's pleasure, then something vital is missing from your life in Christ.

God is visiting this planet today in a way that is virtually unprecedented in secular or Church history. He is touching people in every land, in every culture, and in every circumstance of life. And He is especially touching His Bride, His Church. He is renewing us and calling us back to our first love, Jesus Christ. He is renewing His command that we be ministers of reconciliation, ambassadors of a *better way* to a lost and dying world.

If we answer God's call and lay down everything that has divided us, whether it is racism, theology, philosophy, or gender, then Jesus Christ will unite us as one Church, one Bride, and one blood. If we have the courage to carry the message of reconciliation to our generation, then we will see an international harvest of souls that the ancients could only dream about! I believe that a great harvest is at our doorstep, but as usual God wants us to get up, remove our outer garments of fleshly reputation and division, and begin serving the hungry, the dirty, and the "disqualified" in Jesus' name. The Bridegroom is eager. Is the Bride beginning to sense His passion?

### Endnotes

1. Leanne Payne, *Crisis in Masculinity* (Grand Rapids, Michigan: Baker Books, 1995), 52-69. Originally published in 1985 by Crossway Books.

2. Payne, *Crisis in Masculinity*, 59.

3. Payne, *Crisis in Masculinity*, 60.

4. Payne, *Crisis in Masculinity*, 69-70.

5. James Strong, *Strong's Exhaustive Concordance of the Bible* (Peabody, Massachusetts: Hendrickson Publishers, n.d.), *skubalon* (G2770).

## For more reconciliation resources:

TEACHING SERIES ON RECONCILIATION

| | |
|---|---|
| What Do We Do With the Ministry of Reconciliation?...... | $20.00 |
| Pulling Down the Strongholds of Racism............................. | $20.00 |
| The Model of the Ministry of Reconciliation...................... | $20.00 |

MUSIC TAPES

| | |
|---|---|
| Songs of the Season—Vol I (cassette)................................... | $ 8.00 |
| Songs of the Season—Vol II (cassette) ............................... | $ 8.00 |
| Songs of the Season—Vol I & II (CD) ................................ | $12.00 |
| Maranatha "Live" (cassette)................................................. | $12.00 |
| Maranatha "Live" (CD) ....................................................... | $15.00 |
| Maranatha "Live" (Video)................................................... | $20.00 |
| Solid Rock (cassette)............................................................ | $10.00 |
| Solid Rock (CD) ................................................................. | $12.00 |
| Live Concert (cassette)........................................................ | $ 8.00 |
| I Exalt Thee (cassette) ........................................................ | $ 8.00 |

### Please add appropriate shipping charges:

| | |
|---|---|
| $ 5.00 to $10.00 add...........$2.00 | $50.01 to $60.00 add...........$ 7.00 |
| $10.01 to $20.00 add...........$3.00 | $60.01 to $70.00 add...........$ 8.00 |
| $20.01 to $30.00 add...........$4.00 | $70.01 to $80.00 add...........$ 9.00 |
| $30.01 to $40.00 add...........$5.00 | $80.01 to $90.00 add...........$10.00 |
| $40.01 to $50.00 add...........$6.00 | $90.01 and over, add...........$11.00 |

If you have any questions, call or write:

**Joseph L. Garlington Ministries**
**1111 Wood Street**
**Pittsburgh, PA 15221**
**412-244-9496 (phone) 412-244-9655 (fax)**
**http://www.ccop.org**

Make checks payable to Joseph L. Garlington Ministries. We also accept VISA, MasterCard, American Express, and Discover.

# **D** *Destiny Image*
# New Releases

## WORSHIP: THE PATTERN OF THINGS IN HEAVEN

*by Joseph L. Garlington.*

Joseph Garlington, a favorite Promise Keepers' speaker and worship leader, delves into Scripture to reveal worship and praise from a Heaven's-eye view. Learn just how deep, full, and anointed God intends our worship to be.
ISBN 1-56043-195-4 $9.99p

## WHEN GOD STRIKES THE MATCH

*by Dr. Harvey R. Brown, Jr.*

A noted preacher, college administrator, and father of an "all-American" family—what more could a man want? But when God struck the match that set Harvey Brown ablaze, it ignited a passion for holiness and renewal in his heart that led him into a head-on encounter with the consuming fire of God.
ISBN 0-7684-1000-2 $9.99p

## THE LOST ART OF INTERCESSION

*by Jim W. Goll.*

How can you experience God's anointing power as a result of your own prayer? Learn what the Moravians discovered during their 100-year prayer Watch. They sent up prayers; God sent down His power. Jim Goll, who ministers worldwide through a teaching and prophetic ministry, urges us to heed Jesus' warning to "watch." Through Scripture, the Moravian example, and his own prayer life, Jim Goll proves that "what goes up must come down."
ISBN 1-56043-697-2 $9.99p

## FOR GOD'S SAKE GROW UP!

*by David Ravenhill.*

It's time to grow up...so that we can fulfill God's purposes for us and for our generation! For too long we've been spiritual children clinging to our mother's leg, refusing to go to school on the first day. It's time to put away childish things and mature in the things of God—there is a world that needs to be won to Christ!
ISBN 1-56043-299-3 $9.99p

### Available at your local Christian bookstore.

### Internet: http://www.reapernet.com

Prices subject to change without notice.

# Other *Destiny Image titles* you will enjoy reading

## PRAYER AND FASTING
*by Dr. Kingsley Fletcher.*
We cry, "O God...bring revival to our families, our churches, and our nation."
But we end our prayers quickly—everyone is hungry and we must eat before our
food gets cold. Is it any wonder that our prayers are not prevailing? Discover the
benefits of prayer and fasting...and learn to fast successfully.
ISBN 1-56043-070-2 $9.99p

## IT'S NOT OVER 'TIL IT'S OVER
*by Matthew Ashimolowo.*
Do your circumstances seem overwhelming? Are you tired of feeling earthbound when your heart longs to soar? Does your smile merely hide your
pain? Have you questioned why you were born? Are you wondering how you
can possibly go on? Hang on! Help is on the way! *It's Not Over 'til It's Over!*
ISBN 1-56043-184-9 $8.99p

## IT'S THE WALK NOT THE TALK
*by LaFayette Scales.*
Lots of people talk about spiritual growth, but how many really demonstrate
it? This book outlines and describes six levels of spiritual maturity and
shows you how to move up to the higher levels of God's purpose for His children. Start traveling the path to spiritual maturity in Christ because, after all,
it's the walk, not the talk, that counts!
ISBN 1-56043-170-9 $9.99p

## IS THERE A MAN IN THE HOUSE?
*by Carlton Pearson.*
With passion and eloquence Carlton Pearson calls to men in the Church to heed
God's call to true biblical manhood. Our culture may be confused about man's
role today, but God has never been confused—and His people shouldn't be
either! This wealth of solid, Bible-based counsel will help you transform your
relationships with both men and women!
ISBN 1-56043-270-5 $9.99p

**Available at your local Christian bookstore.**

**Internet: http://www.reapernet.com**

Prices subject to change without notice.

# D *Destiny Image*
# Revival Titles

## SHARE THE FIRE
*by Dr. Guy Chevreau.*

Do you panic when you hear the word *evangelism*? Do you feel awkward "forcing" your opinions on another? All that changes when God abundantly and freely fills you with His Spirit! In *Share the Fire* you'll learn how God has intended evangelism to be: a bold and free work of Christ in you and through you!

ISBN 1-56043-688-3 $9.99p

## THE CHURCH OF THE 3RD MILLENNIUM
*by Marc A. Dupont.*

Uncontrollable laughter, violent shaking, falling "under the Spirit"—can these things really be from God? Using examples from the ministries of Elijah, John the Baptist, and Jesus Himself, Marc Dupont shows that God often moves in ways that challenge traditional religious views or habits; He "offends the mind in order to reveal the heart." God's end-time Church shouldn't be satisfied with the status quo. We need to reach for more of God's Spirit—and not be surprised when He gives it to us!

ISBN 1-56043-194-6 $9.99p

## GO INSIDE THE TORONTO BLESSING—*NEW VIDEO*
*by Warren Marcus.*

Award-winning filmmaker Warren Marcus takes you behind the scenes where you can experience a true look at this revival with footage that has never been filmed before. You will feel like you have a front row seat at the worship services. You will witness the special prayer time when many of the miracles occur. You will see unusual "manifestations"—like those reported in prior revivals. And you will hear first-person account after account of how God has dramatically changed people's lives in this revival.

1 video (approx. 60 min.) ISBN 0-7684-0082-1 Retail $19.99

## Available at your local Christian bookstore.
### Internet: http://www.reapernet.com
Prices subject to change without notice.

# Destiny Image
# New Releases

## BEHOLD THE HARVEST
*by Dale Rumble.*
A final harvest of souls is coming that will be greater than that of all previous revivals! This unique, prophetic study of end-time events reveals how Jesus is going to restore His Church, how children will become warriors in this spiritual army, and many other nuggets of truth!
ISBN 1-56043-192-X $9.99p

## FLASHPOINTS OF REVIVAL
*by Geoff Waugh.*
Throughout history, revival has come to various countries and peoples. Why those times? Why those people? Why not others? This book takes you inside the hearts and minds of people who lived through the major revivals of the past years. Discover how today's revivals fit into God's timeline of awakenings.
ISBN 0-7684-1002-9 $9.99p

## IMAGES OF REVIVAL
*by Richard and Kathryn Riss.*
"Revival" means many things to many people. But what is real revival actually like? In this brief overview, the authors examine the many images of revivals that have occurred throughout the years. God's moves upon His people are exciting and sometimes unexpected. Learn how revival could come to your community!
ISBN 1-56043-687-5 $9.99p

## LET NO ONE DECEIVE YOU
*by Dr. Michael L. Brown.*
No one is knowingly deceived. Everyone assumes it's "the other guy" who is off track. So when people dispute the validity of current revivals, how do you know who is right? In this book Dr. Michael Brown takes a look at current revivals and at the arguments critics are using to question their validity. After examining Scripture, historical accounts of past revivals, and the fruits of the current movements, Dr. Brown comes to a logical conclusion: God's Spirit is moving. *Let No One Deceive You!*
ISBN 1-56043-693-X $10.99p

## Available at your local Christian bookstore.

### Internet: http://www.reapernet.com

Prices subject to change without notice.